Adventures in 3-D

Douglas E. Wolfgram

Adventures in 3-D

Copyright ©1993 by Que® Corporation

All rights reserved. Printed in the United States of America. No part of this book may be used or reproduced in any form or by any means, or stored in a database or retrieval system, without prior written permission of the publisher except in the case of brief quotations embodied in critical articles and reviews. Making copies of any part of this book for any purpose other than your own personal use is a violation of United States copyright laws. For information, address Que Corporation, 11711 N. College Ave., Carmel, IN 46032.

Library of Congress Catalog No.: 93-85250

ISBN: 1-56529-355-X

This book is sold *as is,* without warranty of any kind, either expressed or implied, respecting the contents of this book, including but not limited to implied warranties for the book's quality, performance, merchantability, or fitness for any particular purpose. Neither Que Corporation nor its dealers or distributors shall be liable to the purchaser or any other person or entity with respect to any liability, loss, or damage caused or alleged to be caused directly or indirectly by this book.

96 95 94 93   8 7 6 5 4 3 2 1

Interpretation of the printing code: The rightmost double-digit number is the year of the book's printing; the rightmost single-digit number, the number of the book's printing. For example, a printing code of 93-1 shows that the first printing of the book occurred in 1993.

Screen reproductions in this book were created by the means of the program Collage Plus from Inner Media Inc., Hollis, NH.

Trademarks

All terms mentioned in this book that are known to be trademarks or service marks have been appropriately capitalized. Que cannot attest to the accuracy of this information. Use of a term in this book should not be regarded as affecting the validity of any trademark or service mark.

Dedication

I owe the inspiration and motivation for writing this book to my mentor and friend, Dr. Stephen Erskine. His never-ending enthusiasm for the application of technology to science, specifically medicine, will be an example for generations to come. I can only hope that I am able to pass on what he has taught me about optimism and "keeping one's chin up" to my daughter as she grows up in a world where such attitudes are desperately needed.

Thank you, Stephen.

About the Author
Douglas E. Wolfgram

Douglas E. Wolfgram graduated from Oregon State University in 1979 with a B.S. in Engineering Physics. He soon turned to software development in the fledgling personal computer industry and developed a fast operating system for the Apple II and a 3-D game that resembled the arcade hit *Battle Zone*. In 1982, Wolfgram switched to the IBM PC platform.

He created the first prototype for a painting program on the PC platform and sold it to Mouse Systems. This product became the best-selling paint program on the PC for several years, PC Paint. Wolfgram developed a companion program to PC Paint called Flashgun, which was later sold to Paul Mace Software and marketed under the name of GRASP, or Graphic Animation System for Professionals. GRASP continues to be the platform of choice for DOS presentation development today. Most professional animation and interactive houses use it for product demonstrations and graphic systems prototyping.

Wolfgram is founder and president of GRAFX Group, a leading developer of interactive marketing products. GRAFX provides art and animation services for top computer companies such as NEC, Toshiba, AST, Dell, and Sharp; advertising agencies such as Chiat/Day and Ogilvy Mather; and entertainment giants Paramount Pictures and Universal Studios. Wolfgram also spends a good deal of time writing and speaking to the interactive marketing and multi-media development industries. He is also a sysop of the animation and 3-D forums on CompuServe. He resides in the suburban hills of Southern California with his wife Melody and daughter Paterson Paige.

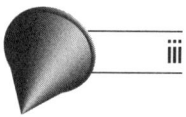

ADVENTURES IN 3-D

Credits

Publisher
　　David Ewing

Associate Publisher
　　Rick Ranucci

Operations Manager
　　Sheila Cunningham

Publishing Plan Manager
　　Thomas H. Bennett

Marketing Manager
　　Ray Robinson

Publishing Manager
　　Joseph B. Wikert

Production Editor
　　Lori Cates

Technical Editor
　　Dan Farmer

Production Manager
　　Corinne Walls

Proofreading/Indexing Coordinator
　　Joelynn Gifford

Production Analyst
　　Mary Beth Wakefield

Illustrations
　　Jodie Cantwell

Book Designer
　　Amy Peppler-Adams

Cover Designer
　　Dean/Johnson Design, Indianapolis

Graphic Image Specialists
　　Dennis Sheehan
　　Susan VandeWalle
　　Tim Montgomery

Production Team
　　Claudia Bell
　　Michelle Greenwalt
　　Heather Kaufman
　　Caroline Roop
　　Michelle Worthington
　　Linda Seifert

Indexer
　　Joy Dean Lee

*Composed in Stone Serif and MCPdigital
by Prentice Hall Computer Publishing*

iv

Acknowledgments

Writing a book is never an easy task. Deadlines mixed with already busy schedules make life uncomfortable for many who surround the author. Primarily, I would like to thank my wife for tolerating the late nights at the office and single-mindedness during delivery deadline time. I would also ask forgiveness of my baby daughter, Paterson, for spending more time at work than at home with her over the last few weeks. Offhand, I'd say an extra trip to Disneyland would be in order, huh Kiddo?

I would like to thank the staff at GRAFX Group for keeping the ship running through the rapids when their fearless leader was off navigating uncharted waters. Hopefully, this experience will help all of us gain new knowledge and experience.

I would also like to thank my support staff at Que. They have been supportive, reliable, and trustworthy during what was a new experience for me, writing an entire book. I will never understand how Lori is able to edit my copy without losing the integrity of emotion expressed in the original, but I am thankful for her gift.

And last, I would like to thank my 12th grade writing teacher, Mr. Harrison, who taught us that there is nothing like a concrete metaphor to make the day go by smoothly. And thanks for unlimited rewrites until we got things right. No pun intended.

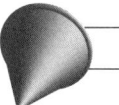

Overview

Introduction 1

Part I Introduction to 3-D Visualization

  1 Human Vision in Three Dimensions 7

  2 The History of 3-D Imaging 27

  3 3-D Images and Viewing Techniques 41

  4 3-D Visualization Applications 57

Part II Using the Computer for 3-D Visualization

  5 3-D Programs and Illusion Techniques 71

  6 Anaglyph Imagery 93

  7 Stereo Imagery on Computer 107

  8 Other 3-D Technologies 121

Part III 3-D Computer Applications

  9 3-D Gaming—Wolfenstein 3-D 137

 10 Hands-on with Vistapro 149

  A Various References on 3-D 185

Index 189

Table of Contents

Introduction 1

I Introduction to 3-D Visualization

1 Human Vision in Three Dimensions   7
The Role of Two Eyes 7
  Visual Cues 8
  Binocular Vision 9
  Experience and Relative Size 11
  Scope 14
  Perspective 15
  Other Cues 18
The Anatomy of the Eye 19
  The Structure of the Eye 20
  Problems 21
  Accommodation and Convergence 21
  Retinal Disparity and Other Myths 22
Why Some People Cannot See in 3-D 23
  Impaired Vision 24
  Color Blindness 24
  Environmental Conditions 25
  Bad Luck 26
Summary 26

2 The History of 3-D Imaging   27
The First Stereoscopes 27
  Sir Charles Wheatstone's Reflecting Stereoscope 27
  Lens Stereoscopes 28
  Modern Reflecting Stereoscopes 32
  The Kaiser Panorama 34
Early 3-D Photographs and Cameras 34
Viewmaster 36
Modern Stereo Cameras 37
Nimslo Lenticular Photography 38
Summary 39

3 3-D Images and Viewing Techniques   41
Stereo Pairs 41
  Relaxed Stereo Viewing 42
  Stereoscopic Viewers 45
  Random-Dot Stereograms 47
Anaglyph Imagery 48
Polarized 3-D Images 50
Holographic Images 52
The Pulfrich Effect 54
Summary 56

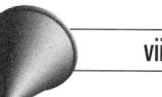

4 3-D Visualization Applications   57
Aerial Photogrammetry 57
Medicine 58
Architecture 61
Military 62
Entertainment 62
Biology 64
Space 66
Summary 67

II Using the Computer for 3-D Visualization

5 3-D Programs and Illusion Techniques   71
Translating 3-D into 2-D 72
Shading Models 77
    Flat Shading 77
    Gouraud Shading 79
    Phong Shading 80
    Diffuse and Specular Reflection 82
Shadows 83
Other Properties 84
Ray Tracing 84
Other Surface Details 87
Environmental Effects 91
Summary 92

6 Anaglyph Imagery   93
Anaglyphs on a Computer Screen 94
Viewing Some Anaglyphs 95
Making an Anaglyph 97
    Techniques for 3-D Programs 97
    Designing for Anaglyphs 97
    Making Your Own Anaglyphs with Anadraw 98
Animating Anaglyphs 103
Summary 106

7 Stereo Imagery on Computer   107
Graphics Hardware 107
    The Development of Adequate Computer
    Graphics Hardware 108
    Resolution and Loss of Information 108
Stereo Output from 3-D Programs 110
    Stereo Separation 111
Hands-on Examples 112
    Viewing Some Stereo Pairs 112
    Drawing in Stereo 114
Hardware Stereo Viewing Devices 117
    LCD Shutter Glasses 118
    StereoGraphics Crystal Eyes 119
Summary 119

8 Other 3-D Technologies — 121
Fractals 121
    Background and History 121
    Fractal Technology for Real-Life Simulations 124
Virtual Reality.. 127
    Background and History 127
    VR on a Computer 128
    VR for VR's Sake..................................... 128
    Making "Sense" of it All 129
    Input and Output 129
    Applications... 131
Summary 132

III 3-D Computer Applications

9 3-D Gaming—Wolfenstein 3-D — 137
Technology... 137
The Story So Far...(from the Wolfenstein Player's Manual) 138
    Starting the Game 139
    Movement 140
    Arms 141
    Killing the Enemy 141
    Doors 141
    Stuff 142
    The Next Floor 142
    The Status Screen 144
    Bad Guys 145
    Hints 146
Summary 146

10 Hands-on with Vistapro — 149
Installing the Software on Your System...................... 149
    Basic Requirements 150
What Is Vistapro?... 150
    What You Can Do with Vistapro 150
    Where Vistapro Gets Its Data 151
    What Is Vistapro Used For?........................... 151
    Getting the Most Out of Vistapro 152
Getting Started—Your First Fractal Landscape 152
Back to Basics—The Vistapro Menus 155
    The Project Menu 155
    The Load and Save Menus 155
    The GrMode Menu 155
    The Script and ImpExp Menus 155
    The IQ Menu 156
Tutorial 1—Selecting a View 156
    Setting Your Target 156
    Setting the Camera 157
    The *P* button for Perspective Viewing 159
    Bank, Head, Pitch, and Range 160

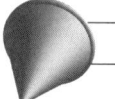

Tutorial 2—Adding Objects to Your Vistapro World............. 162
    Sea Level, Tree Line, Snow Line, and Haze Density 162
    Sky, Horizn, Valley, and Cliffs........................... 164
    Lakes and Rivers..................................... 165
    Stars 168
    Tree 168
    Clouds 170
    VScale, Enlarg, Shrink, and Smooth 172
    NumClr, RGBPal, LckPal, and CMap.................... 173
Improving the Rendering................................. 176
    Main.. 176
    Lens 178
    Frac... 180
    Light.. 182
Summary 183

A Various References on 3-D   185

Organizations 185
Catalog of 3-D Products 186
Books on 3-D and Computer Graphics 187

Index... 189

Introduction

We live in a three-dimensional world, yet we often find ourselves trying to analyze it using a two-dimensional device—the computer. This book introduces you to various techniques for visualizing objects in three dimensions on a computer display. Using special display technology, custom hardware, and subtle tricks, we can fool our eyes into believing that we are seeing three dimensions. Sometimes, we can even do a good enough job of tricking our eyes to perform comprehensive diagnostic analysis, make critical medical decisions, and formulate strategic military plans. We use this information to educate, inform, and entertain.

As with many other parts of the human body, we often take our eyes for granted. We have a doctor check them every once in a while, and we try to protect them from injury. If our vision is impaired, we use corrective lenses, but we take for granted the 24-hour-a-day job they perform for us. They watch where we walk. They observe who we interact with. They take note of the time of day. They detect the color of a rose, and even burn a little when there is too much pollen in the air. At the speed of light, information rushes through the pupils and into our heads, where our brains process it. We continue to process endlessly from pre-dawn rapid eye movement to the last minute of the late show, all without even knowing what is really going on within our eyes. We learn about rays of light, the cornea, the lens, and the retina in elementary school, but no one ever stops to explain one of the real mysteries of vision and the world in which we live: our perception of three dimensions.

In 1884, Edwin Abbott taught us a better appreciation for our 3-D world by writing a classic mathematical novel, *Flatland*. In *Flatland*, we are led through the often-complex life of beings who exist in a two-dimensional world. Flatland's inhabitants are shapes with one or more sides. At the bottom of the social spectrum are women, who exist only as straight lines, or single-sided polygons.

As a Flatlander moves up the class ladder, he gets more sides. The middle class is made up of doctors and lawyers, who are squares and pentagons. The most important people are kings and monarchs, whose sides are so plentiful that they resemble circles. The Flatlanders' houses and other buildings are always pentagons. They have natural landmarks such as rocks and trees, but all appear as single lines.

The problem in the world of Flatland is that from a two-dimensional perspective, everyone and everything looks like a straight line. The Flatlanders are clever, though, and from a very early age they learn to distinguish between inhabitants by noticing how quickly their sides fade away into the ever-present fog. A triangle (working class) has much steeper sides than a pentagon, so his sides recede faster and he is immediately recognizable. Because the Flatlanders do not enjoy our 3-D point of view, namely, a top view, they have devised tricks to fool their singular eye (they have no need for two eyes, because 3-D vision is not a requirement) into thinking it sees something it doesn't—depth.

Back in the world of three dimensions, we depend on 3-D information to make decisions about every waking moment. How big is that step? How deep is that river? How far away is that traffic sign? How tall is that building? Is that my car being towed away down the street? Engineers, geographers, cartographers, doctors, and scientists all use three-dimensional information to make important decisions that affect our daily lives. They also use computers in their jobs, so it makes sense that they try to use these computers to process their three-dimensional data.

A computer display is flat, so we need tricks and gimmicks to fool our eyes into thinking they are looking at three dimensions. Like the Flatlanders, we find ourselves to be extremely resourceful in this area. With *Adventures in 3-D*, you can explore some of these tricks in detail, as well as gain hands-on experience creating your own original 3-D worlds.

This book is divided into three parts. Part I is dedicated to understanding how 3-D (binocular) vision works. In it, you learn the basics of eye anatomy and why you need two eyes to see in 3-D. Part II investigates several methods of using a computer to work with three dimensions, including anaglyph imagery, stereo pairs, and rendering techniques such as shadows and shading. Part III is dedicated to the curious child in all of us. In it, you explore the world of virtual reality in a 3-D game, and generate realistic landscapes using fractal technology. All topics are supported with hands-on computer software tools. After reading this book and experimenting with the software, you will have a greater knowledge and understanding of the 3-D world.

As computers get faster and less expensive, 3-D applications will become as commonplace as Nintendo game machines and television sets. Data and information will be represented in holographic simulations. The entire three-dimensional world around us will be embedded inside the computers in front of us.

With any luck, we will come full circle and take it all for granted... again.

Part I

Introduction to 3-D Visualization

Human Vision in Three Dimensions

No one knows for certain whether the cyclopes really existed. Greek mythology tells of three such creatures who were the sons of Gaea and Uranus. These three unusual giants were unique in that they had only one eye. Apparently, this didn't stop them from performing their tasks: making Zeus' thunderbolts, Poseidon's trident, and Hades' invisibility cap.

Homer tells of a huge, one-eyed shepherd who lived in a rocky cave and had a run-in with Odysseus and his men. The gallant men on Odysseus's ship finally won the battle by blinding the monocular giant with a hot, sharp tree trunk.

The Role of Two Eyes

Both fables leave many questions unanswered about exactly how the cyclopes may have lived. One thing we do know, however, is that if they did exist and their brains were similar to a human's, they wouldn't have seen very well in this three-dimensional world of ours. To be able to see in three dimensions requires the input

1 INTRODUCTION TO 3-D VISUALIZATION

from two properly functioning eyes. The input from a cyclops' singular optical receptor would have severely limited his ability to do battle. For a brain to perceive three dimensions, image data from two independent sources with slightly different points of view are combined, and the ever-so-slight differences are analyzed and noted. These differences tell the brain that one object is farther away than another. This process of combining and analyzing two images into one three-dimensional image is known as *binocular vision* or *stereoscopic vision*. It was also referred to as a *cyclopean image* in the early days of stereo photography.

The fundamental benefit of binocular vision is called *depth perception*. From the time we are old enough to cross the street by ourselves, we are taught to look both ways before crossing. But without the ability to properly judge the distance of the oncoming cars, this gesture is of little value. Depth perception enables us to gauge distance in a relative sense with a remarkable degree of accuracy. It is doubtful whether the cyclopes had the keen depth perception of their two-eyed adversaries.

Visual Cues

The other main component required to perceive three dimensions is relative knowledge and experience. By comparing an unfamiliar object in a scene with a point of reference either in our field of view or in our memory, another set of "cues" emerges, which help determine an object's position and size in three-dimensional space. If you look around your desktop, you will probably see a paper clip, a pencil, or a stapler, all of which are familiar objects. If an unfamiliar object such as a small gemstone you have never seen before is thrown into the foray, you are able to make an immediate judgment as to its size, *relative* to the other objects. Your experience with the familiar objects enables you to quickly draw a conclusion about the new one.

This might be where the cyclops had an advantage. If his life span were longer than that of a human, his experiences would be more extensive, thus enhancing his ability to make quick judgments regarding the positioning of objects in the world around him. Other visual experience cues include shading, shadowing, and environmental effects such as fog and light intensity.

HUMAN VISION IN THREE DIMENSIONS

At times, it is difficult to distinguish between stereoscopic effects and visual cues or *monocular effects*. At a great distance, objects appear flat whether you use one eye or two. The real benefits of stereoscopic vision are realized at distances around 6 to 10 feet. This will become more clear as you learn more about exactly how humans see in three dimensions. When you look at the examples along the way, keep the viewing distance in mind when you are deciding exactly which factors are contributing to the 3-D effect you are experiencing.

Binocular Vision

The basis of three-dimensional vision lies in using two independently captured images from slightly separated points of view (see fig. 1.1). The brain processes and interprets these images, and makes all the calculations needed to determine the relative position of the objects in the scene using information from the images.

Many factors contribute to the quality of three-dimensional vision. The distance between the eyes, the quality of the image, the ability of the eyes to focus each image, the speed at which the image is focused, and the general health of the viewer's nervous system all contribute to the analysis process. A complete treatise on human anatomy is beyond the scope of this book, but it is important to understand that the overall process of vision is one of the most complex human attributes.

The distance between our eyes is set by nature and there isn't much we can do about it. Because our brains develop vision as we develop and grow, any compensation needed by the brain to accommodate abnormal eye separation is done automatically. For point of discussion, the average interpupillary separation for adult males is 65 to 66 millimeters. Women average 2 to 3 millimeters less. Children reach an interpupillary separation of 55 millimeters by the age of 10. Although this is not incredibly important to normal vision, it has a lot to do with building stereoscopic viewing devices.

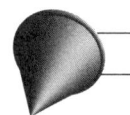

1 INTRODUCTION TO 3-D VISUALIZATION

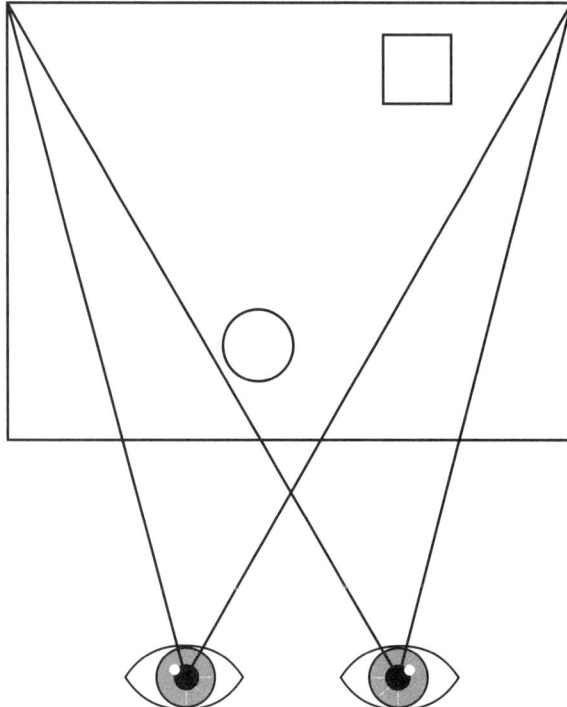

Figure 1.1

A binocular vision diagram.

Image Quality

The quality of the image we see is also an important factor contributing to our ability to perceive three dimensions. The eyes must be able to focus the image properly so that a relative distance marker is established. If the images we receive are fuzzy or out of focus, establishing this marker is difficult. Some causes of problem images are dirty glasses, faulty eyesight, rapidly moving images that are difficult to focus, and atmospheric conditions that inhibit vision. The link between the eye and the brain is not short. If any part of the nervous system that lies in that connecting path is faulty, it can affect our ability to see properly. There are many nervous system conditions that apply here, but they are beyond the scope of this discussion.

HUMAN VISION IN THREE DIMENSIONS

Registration Point

In general, objects in a given scene *converge* at a particular point in the distance. This point is referred to as the *registration point*. Look at figure 1.2. The registration point in this pair of images is the back of the rectangular "floor" (the large rectangle in fig. 1.1). On the left side is the image seen by the left eye, and on the right side is that seen by the right eye. Notice that the sphere appears larger than the cube. Notice also that the sphere is closer to the left edge in the right-eye image than it is in the left-eye image. The brain takes note of this and determines that the sphere is fairly close to our eyes relative to the registration point (this distance is labeled A_1 and A_2 in figure 1.2). The separation of the cubes is far less, and therefore exists at the "back" of the image (this separation distance is labeled B_1 and B_2).

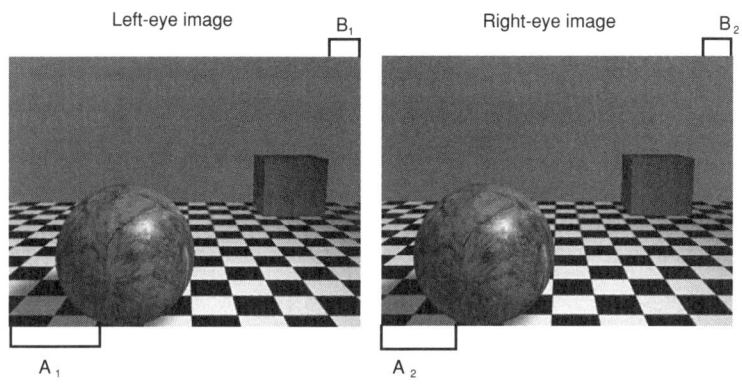

Note that $A_1 > A_2$, whereas B_1 is about the same as B_2.

Figure 1.2
Left- and right-eye views.

Now look at the floor. You will note the squares getting smaller as they go toward the "back" of the image. This is yet another cue. A discussion of visual cues follows, but for now note the differences between the images that are related to the object placement within the image. These differences tell the brain how the scene is composed.

Experience and Relative Size

Size is a relative term. When referring to figure 1.2, I said that the sphere *appears* larger than the cube. In real-world coordinates, they have the same diameter. Because the sphere is closer to us than the cube, it appears larger.

1 INTRODUCTION TO 3-D VISUALIZATION

Figure 1.3 shows a box sitting by itself. Without the aid of a visual cue, you have no way of telling how large the object really is. Notice also that the box is labeled *Contents: Books*. Although this label in itself isn't conclusive, you can determine something about the size of the box. What you don't know is exactly how many books are inside the box and what size they are.

Figure 1.3

A simple box.

Your knowledge of books gives you an indication of a possible range of sizes for the box. If the box were labeled *Contents: Sofa*, you would have a totally different impression of its size. From the time you were born and opened your eyes for the first time, you began gathering a huge database of information that you will use the rest of your life as visual aids. This database tells you that a box containing books is probably smaller than a box containing a sofa.

Now look at figure 1.4. It is the same box sitting on the porch of a house. The house in the background gives you some indication as to how large or how close the box might be. Notice the size of the window. Some impression of the size of a normal window ("normal" is in itself a relative term) hits you and thus, you are able to draw an even better-supported conclusion about the size of the box. Although it still is not entirely conclusive, you have more information than in the first example (fig. 1.3) and feel more comfortable surmising the box's size.

Think for a moment about the following objects and how they relate in terms of size: a kitten, the house you grew up in, the street you lived on, the neighbor's dog, members of your family, and the family car. These images are some of the first you encountered, and yet today they still are useful references.

HUMAN VISION IN THREE DIMENSIONS

Figure 1.4

The simple box in a familiar scene.

Experience is an entirely personal thing. You cannot share it with anyone. Here's a further illustration. Let's say your mother is standing next to a stranger. The stranger's head extends a good distance above your mother's. To the casual passerby who has no knowledge of your mother's size, the only determination that he can make is that your mother is shorter than the stranger (assuming, of course, that we give the observer no other visual cues he may be familiar with, such as a standard-sized front door). Armed with the intimate knowledge that your mother is six feet tall, you can also make the determination that the stranger is "tall." Our observer might draw the conclusion that your mother is short, or that the stranger is tall, but only with the proper reference material can an absolute determination be made. The passerby can conclude only that which his own experience supports.

1 INTRODUCTION TO 3-D VISUALIZATION

Scope

Just how far away is the sailboat in figure 1.5? There is no way of determining, because you have no data about the size of the boat, and the sea is so large that in this view, it appears to be infinite. The waves themselves provide no point of reference, because experience tells you that waves come in many sizes. But if you pull back just a little (fig. 1.6), you see that the boat is not on the sea at all—it's a toy boat in a bathtub.

Figure 1.5

A sailboat on the water.

This illustrates another important point about three-dimensional viewing. Our eyes are limited in scope just as the boundaries of the page in this book limit the size of the figures. We never see the entire world around us all at once. If we did, we would have a much better database from which to gather the reference materials for proper analytical viewing. Even though it sometimes appears as though we have enough information to properly process an image, errors occur. There is no way to be sure exactly when we have all the information necessary to make a perfectly accurate judgment, but that is one of the games of life. The more information you have, the better the probability that you can draw a correct conclusion.

HUMAN VISION IN THREE DIMENSIONS

Figure 1.6

A sailboat in a bathtub.

Often, we find ourselves totally fooled by what we see. This is referred to as *optical illusion*. There are many famous optical illusions, and just as famous are the optical illusionists who create them. M.C. Escher is well-known for his drawings of three-dimensional objects and environments that cannot possibly exist in the real world. What fools us is that small portions of his drawings look real. It is only when viewed as a whole that they become fantasy. Again, we must ask ourselves if we have enough information to draw the proper conclusions.

Perspective

Figure 1.7 shows a cube drawn in *isometric* style and the same box drawn with *perspective*. Perspective drawing is a technique developed by architects to more accurately illustrate the depth of their drawings. Perspective is a difficult concept to describe with words, but with a simple illustration it becomes clear.

Look at figure 1.8. The lines that frame your field of view are not parallel lines. They form an angle. This angle of view varies slightly from individual to individual. The ability to see things at the edge

1 INTRODUCTION TO 3-D VISUALIZATION

of one's field of view is called *peripheral vision*. Some people have better peripheral vision than others. Usually, this is because their eyes react very quickly to movement and are able to change focus rapidly so that when something moves in the "corner of their eye," their brains react to it immediately. For those of us with more slowly focusing eyes, this capability is slightly limited.

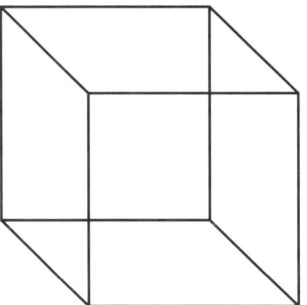
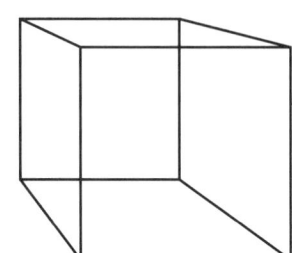

Figure 1.7

Isometric and perspective drawing.

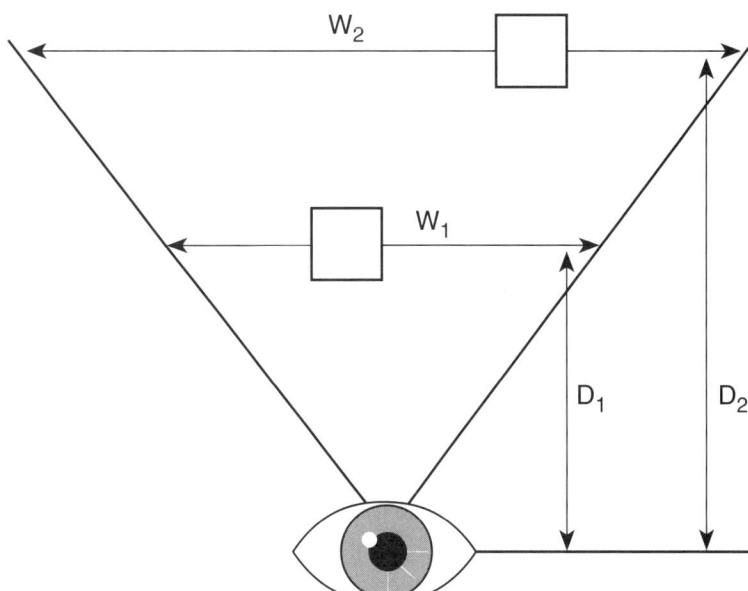

Figure 1.8

The field of view.

HUMAN VISION IN THREE DIMENSIONS

It is easy to see from figure 1.8 (in which D_1 and D_2 are the distance to the object from the viewer's eye) that the farther away an object is, the smaller it appears in your field of view. This concept extends to infinity, theoretically. A point placed at infinity is infinitely small. Differential calculus also tells us that an extremely large object placed at infinity will be infinitely small. If an object is placed close to you, it occupies more of your field of view than it would were it placed farther away. If the back of an object is significantly farther away from you than the front, it will have diminished enough to be noticeably smaller.

The back of the cube in the center of figure 1.9a is completely hidden from view by the front of the cube. If we move the cube over in our field of view (fig. 1.9b), we see the effect of perspective.

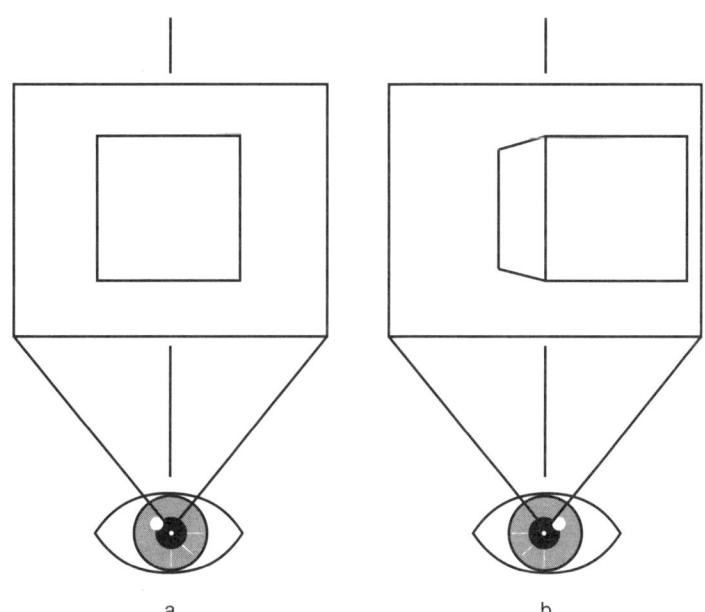

a   b

Figure 1.9

One-point perspective.

The lines that connect the front and the back of the cube in figure 1.9b are converging toward each other. Where they meet is the registration point or point of convergence, as mentioned previously. This type of drawing is called *one-point perspective*, because all lines along the sight line converge into a single point. This is a relatively easy drawing format; all the architect or artist has to do is draw a single point somewhere and have all new lines parallel to the line of sight coverge to it.

1 INTRODUCTION TO 3-D VISUALIZATION

In a drawing and illustration, this point does not necessarily have to lie in the field of view. As a point of contrast, isometric drawing means that all parts of all objects are drawn as though they are in the same plane (see fig. 1.10). Notice that the front of the cube in figure 1.10 is the same size as the back. This type of drawing lacks the realism that is present in perspective drawing, but is useful when detail is more important than realism. An example of this is machine parts catalogs or instructional assembly diagrams. In both cases, it is more important for the viewer to see all elements of the object than to project it into 3-D space in a realistic manner.

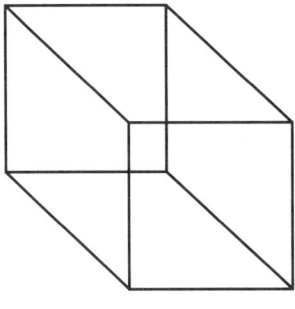

Figure 1.10

Isometric cubes.

Other Cues

In addition to relative size, scope, and perspective, there are other cues you learn to depend on for making decisions about what you see. You know that the sun shines from overhead, and that objects that lie between the sun and other objects cast shadows. When the sun is shining from behind you, an object in front of you casts a shadow that recedes away from you. This isn't necessarily an indication of size and distance in an absolute sense, but it is a sign that three dimensions exist.

Logic (as well as experience) tells you that the side of an object is lit more brightly on the side that is closer to the source of the light. Shaded areas and brightly lit areas of an object are indications of its 3-D nature. You might remember from the introduction that the people of Edwin Abbott's *Flatland* used their ever-present fog to calculate distance in two dimensions.

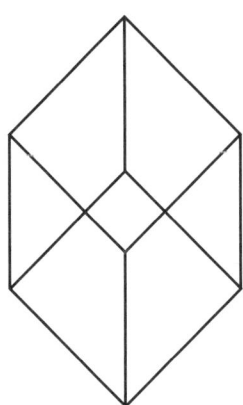

HUMAN VISION IN THREE DIMENSIONS

We too have fog and haze, although it is not as predictable as in *Flatland*. Objects that lie on the horizon are faded and washed out compared to objects that are close to us. The sky is darker straight above our head than anywhere else. If an object is not directly aligned with our line of sight, its perspective might be difficult to recognize.

Imagine a non-rectangular object such as a coffee cup. If the cup is sitting still, it may be difficult to get a feel for the perspective it casts. But if it is rotating in space, our brains detect the changing perspective and immediately conclude that it is in fact a 3-D object.

A ball rotating in space is difficult to analyze because the highlights, shading, and shadows do not change as it spins. But the corners of a spinning cube make its existence in three dimensions obvious. To properly detect a spinning sphere, we rely on subtle changes in surface texture and the way they reflect light. If it is a perfectly smooth, perfectly colored, non-reflecting ball in flat light, there is no way to tell that it is three-dimensional, even when it spins. In these cases, we depend on nonvisual cues such as the noise it might make while it spins. If experience tells us that this object shouldn't normally be making any noise, we get suspicious and draw the conclusion that perhaps it is moving.

The case of a sphere is an interesting one. A perfect sphere is the ultimate three-dimensional object. From any angle, it looks like a circle. Even shadows and shading are not conclusive. A circle can be painted to look like a sphere. Fog can be painted onto its receding edges. Fortunately, we don't often encounter spheres in situations where no other visual cues exist.

The Anatomy of the Eye

Most of us learned as early as the sixth grade about the cornea, pupil, lens, and optic nerve, and how light enters the eye and we see an upside-down image on the back of the eyeball. But that was the extent of our learning. We always assumed that what we saw was one image. We never stopped to think about the fact that each eye receives a different image. It all happens so quickly that to us it always looked like one image and we just figured that was the way things were and everything was working properly. We were never

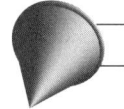

1 INTRODUCTION TO 3-D VISUALIZATION

told why we need two eyes to see properly in a 3-D world. We were never told about the particular components of the eye that contribute to 3-D vision.

The Structure of the Eye

Many things about the eye and its components contribute to the quality and the ability of vision. To gather a better understanding of the entire process, let's start at the beginning. At the outside of the eye, the eyelid protects and lubricates the cornea (see fig. 1.11). The cornea acts as a shield to protect the eye and begins the vision process by refracting or bending the light toward the pupil. The pupil is the opening in the iris through which all light enters the eye.

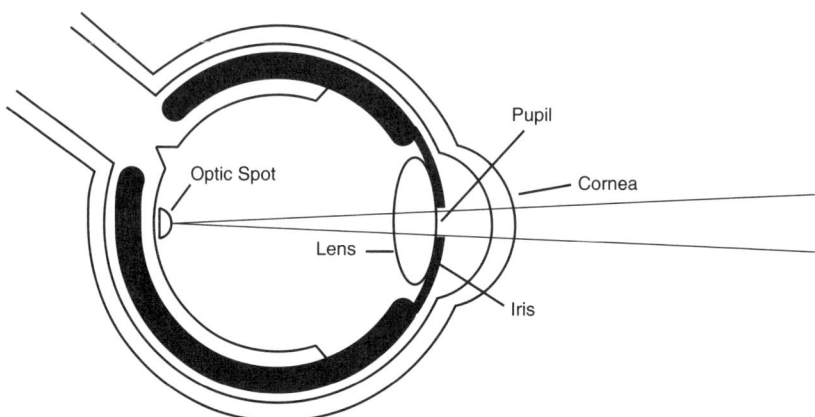

Figure 1.11

The fundamental anatomy of the eye.

As the light passes through the pupil, it is again refracted by the lens, which focuses the rays onto the back of the eyeball. A variety of fluids and muscles aid in the process along the way as well. There are six pairs of small muscles which keep the eyes aligned and parallel.

Finally, at the back of the eye, the optic nerve endings come together into what is called the *retina*. The image is gathered up by the optic nerve and passed along toward the brain. The optic nerve

HUMAN VISION IN THREE DIMENSIONS

enters the underside of the brain at a region called the *lateral geniculate body*. Some degree of information processing occurs here, but the remainder of analysis is done when it reaches the *visual cortex*.

Interestingly enough, the upside-down, left-eye image is processed in the right half of the brain, and the upside-down, right-eye image is processed in the left half. What results is a single image that is right-side up! It is unclear exactly how much processing of the image is done along the way, but it is known that humans as a species process more in their brains than some other species. Frogs, for example, do much of their visual processing in the eyeball itself.

Problems

If any of the steps in the process of vision is not carried out in perfect succession and without flaw, the entire process suffers. Corneal problems cause the rays to be refracted incorrectly. Misshapen eyeballs cause difficulty in focusing. Tired muscles inhibit the ability of the lens to properly focus the rays onto the retina. If there are no problems in either eye, the brain gets what it needs to begin the process of 3-D vision—two clear, parallel images.

Accommodation and Convergence

The two words most commonly used to describe the process that our eyes go through in seeing stereoscopically are *accommodation* and *convergence*. Accommodation is like focusing a camera. To vary its focal length, the lens of the eye is made thicker or flatter by the muscles that surround it. With a camera, the lens moves in or out relative to the iris. This is because the shape of the lens of a camera is fixed, so to change its focal length, you must change its distance from the pupil.

Convergence is the movement of the eyeballs so that the optic axes of both eyes converge at the same point. Convergence and accommodation usually work together in normal vision. If you hold your finger in front of you at arm's length, then move it quickly to a position halfway to your nose, your eyes will both move and refocus. These two operations are not necessarily linked, however,

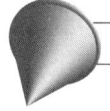

I INTRODUCTION TO 3-D VISUALIZATION

and the intentional unlinking is a good way to resolve stereo images, as you will see later.

Retinal Disparity and Other Myths

Early stereoscopic theorists had many incorrect assumptions about how we see in three dimensions. The most famous is the myth of *retinal disparity*. Although retinal disparity does exist, its contribution to 3-D viewing was misunderstood for some time. Figure 1.12 shows how the theory evolved. Points a, b, and c are successive points along the field of view.

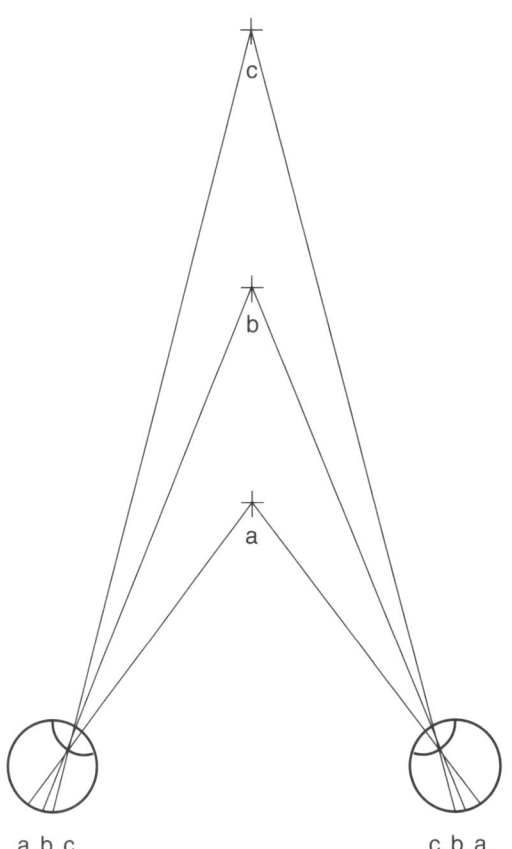

Figure 1.12
A retinal disparity diagram.

If you focus (*converge*) strongly on point b, the place where the image hits the retina is b_1 in the left eye and b_2 in the right eye. Accordingly, points a and c will be collected at points a_1, c_1 and a_2, c_2, respectively.

The basis of the early theory was that we did all the processing in our eyes at the optic nerve ending, or *fovea centralis* (also referred to as the *yellow spot*). If this were true, we could measure the difference or disparity of retinal images and know that *a* was in front of *b* and that *c* was behind it. Many later experiments proved this theory wrong, but optically, it made sense at the time.

Another early theory said that *monocular zones* are the cause of stereoscopic viewing. Monocular zones are the regions that are visible only by one eye as a result of the displacement of the eyeballs. A simple way to think of it is this: Imagine yourself standing at the corner of a building. You put your nose along the edge of the building so that your right eye sees the brick wall of the building and the left eye sees down the alley. Obviously, each eye sees a totally different image.

Look again at figure 1.2. If the sphere overlapped the cube, it is easy to see that the right eye would see portions of the left side of the cube that would be hidden from the view of the left eye by the sphere. In other words, the right eye sees "behind" the sphere into regions that the left eye cannot. In any case, this theory was disproved by the invention of *random-dot stereograms* by Bela Julez. I discuss random-dot stereograms more in Chapter 2.

Why Some People Cannot See in 3-D

In spite of all that has been said about how humans see in 3-D, some unlucky souls are simply not able to perceive three dimensions. No matter how hard they try, they cannot gather enough information to properly assess the situation and draw three-dimensional conclusions about it. The degree of their inability

1 INTRODUCTION TO 3-D VISUALIZATION

varies, depending on several factors. Impaired vision, environmental factors, and just plain bad luck all contribute to their 3-D vision problems.

Impaired Vision

Some unlucky souls are stricken with cyclops syndrome. These people include those blind or nearly blind in one eye and those with *amblyopia*, sometimes referred to as *lazy eye*. The condition of lazy eye means that one eye focuses much more slowly than the other. When this happens, the good eye gets tired of waiting for the slow eye to catch up, so the brain just uses the signals from the good eye. The result is that over a period of time, the person gets used to single-eye viewing. People with this condition cannot resolve three dimensions. They rely on the other visual cues that we spoke of, namely references and experience.

Those unfortunate people with night blindness have a difficult enough time getting around after dark. At the back of the eye are *rods* which act as low-intensity light receptors. If someone has poorly functioning rods, they are said to be night blind. Their lack of light reception inhibits 3-D vision much more severely than that of normally sighted people.

The converse of night blindness is poorly functioning *cones*. Cones are the high-intensity receptors. Poorly functioning cones create a condition called snow-blindness. If all light above a certain threshold of intensity is pushed to white, the surroundings are washed out, much like being caught in a blinding blizzard.

Color Blindness

One factor which has gone unspoken of until this point is the contribution that color makes to three-dimensional viewing. Color consists of both saturation and hue, and experience tells us that unsaturated parts of an object may be farther away than the brightly colored parts. If these differences lie in a color which the viewer cannot perceive, these subtleties may be indistinguishable, therefore making the object look flat.

Certain objects that we use for relative sizing or experience measurements have a different meaning to someone who is color-blind. At a distance, an apple looks a lot like a grape if one is not able to perceive their respective colors. If just one of these objects is used for a relative-size conclusion, problems arise.

Color-blind people learn from an early age to distinguish objects in ways that those of us with normal sight cannot even imagine, but there exists an overall disability in them that creates great difficulty in particular situations. Adjacent colors which are the same intensity still provide depth for people with normal color perception. One object lies completely in front of the other if it is entirely in view. But a red apple on a large green leaf may disappear to a color-blind person. If there is no shadow or other edge indicator, the objects merge into one shape.

Environmental Conditions

The contrast of our daytime world goes away at night. Without light, many subtleties disappear. Shadows are less obvious. Shading becomes flat. Highlights are nothing more than flat surfaces. On cloudy days, the lighting is much flatter, and again the contrast that aids us with highlights and shadows is diminished. Any time that the light becomes flat, our world gets flatter. Those with already impaired 3-D vision suffer even more. If normal daytime vision is difficult, imagine the complexities that arise when the visual cues they have learned to depend on are diminished as well.

A good example of a field that is hard-hit by poor atmospheric conditions is the world of professional sports. Baseball players have a difficult time judging fly balls during night games and cloudy days. Golfers have a difficult time picking the right club when distance to the pin is reduced to a guessing game during the twilight hours. Tennis players often mis-time service returns when the lighting isn't right.

I INTRODUCTION TO 3-D VISUALIZATION

Bad Luck

After all that has been said about the world of 3-D and the possible problems associated with perceiving it, there is one statistic which we cannot overlook. Approximately five percent of people with normal vision cannot perceive 3-D. No one knows why. It is a clinically measured statistic which overrides anything we can say about seeing in a three-dimensional world. Those people who are part of this group have nothing on which to blame their misfortune but simple bad luck.

Summary

The human experience of seeing in three dimensions is truly a marvel. As beings with two parallel yet independent eyes, we have the ability to observe subtle aberrations in the cyclopean image sent to our brain via the optic nerve. This ability, called binocular vision, is not prevalent among all animal species. A chameleon, for example, hardly ever has his two eyes in parallel, so binocular vision is impossible. In addition, our life spans provide years for gathering valuable experience. This experience, along with rational thought, enables us to make decisions about what we see in a relative sense. Comparing objects in a scene provides conclusive information about their size and placement.

For most people, everyday life is filled with a dependence on 3-D eyesight. Walking down the street, preparing dinner, driving a car, or participating in a sporting event are all easier with a good perception of three dimensions. Although it is possible to function without it (as many blind people do every day), 3-D vision is a basic and wondrous part of our human existence.

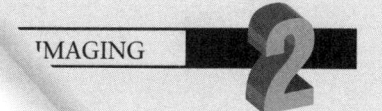

The History of 3-D Imaging

The First Stereoscopes

Although 3-D imaging on the computer is a relatively new topic, stereo imagery in general has been common since the last century. In this chapter, we explore some of the great moments in 3-D image history. This chapter also looks at the development of stereo equipment and where technology has taken us.

Sir Charles Wheatstone's Reflecting Stereoscope

As you learned in the first chapter, the basis for viewing in three dimensions is taking two independent planar images and restricting the viewing environment so that one image is viewed by the left eye and the other image is viewed by the right eye. The brain does the rest of the work. Sir Charles Wheatstone is credited with inventing the first stereoscope around 1838. It was a reflecting stereoscope, as shown in figure 2.1.

I INTRODUCTION TO 3-D VISUALIZATION

Figure 2.1

Wheatstone's reflecting stereoscope.

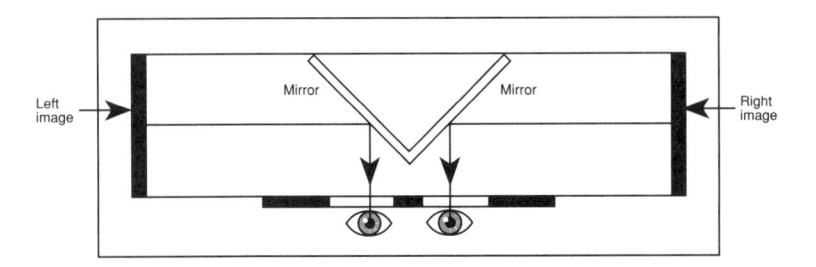

In the early days of photography, it was difficult to generate high-quality photographs in small format, so a lens stereoscope that did not permit large-format viewing simply wouldn't work.

Wheatstone used mirrors at 45-degree angles to reflect the opposing images toward the openings where the viewer placed his eyes. There was a slot into which the viewer placed his nose for comfort. There was, however, a slight problem with this device. Closer inspection reveals that because the images are reflected from mirrors, they are optically reversed. An easy fix is to put the left image on the right side of the device and the right image on the left side.

Various enhancements and additions to this technology have been made, but the Wheatstone device is still the most popular for viewing photo negatives and x-rays. What made Wheatstone's invention unique among stereoscopes was its lack of lenses. Because the images were reflected from mirrors, all the user had to be concerned with was properly placing and aligning the images so that the viewer obtained a full view. Later, lens-assisted devices became popular because they could be adjusted to correct for varying image size and viewer eye separation.

Lens Stereoscopes

Light entering a positive lens from an infinite distance (light rays are parallel upon entering) is focused at a single point. This is called the *focal point* of the lens.

THE HISTORY OF 3-D IMAGING

Light entering the lens at an angle (from the focal point) is refracted so that it is parallel to the line of sight when it reaches the eye (see fig. 2.2). This is just one case of light behavior through positive lenses, but it is the most important one as far as stereoscopy is concerned. This knowledge can be used to successfully separate images for stereo viewing. If either the inside half (fig. 2.3a) or outside half (fig. 2.3b) is used exclusively, the light is isolated.

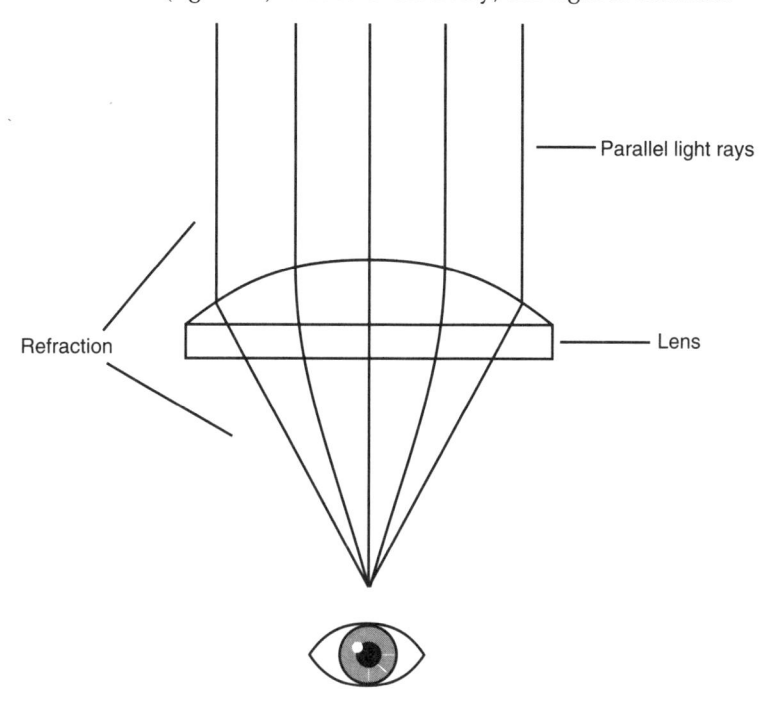

Figure 2.2

Positive lens optics.

For the method described in figure 2.3a, the centers of the pupils must be closer together than the images, whereas in 2.3b, the images must be closer together. Of course, we cannot adjust our interpupillary separation, so the images must be adjusted.

The preferable method of stereo viewing is that illustrated in figure 2.3a. Because the light is coming from a wider separation than the eyes, there are two benefits. The first is that because the light (image) separation is greater, we can use larger images. The other benefit is that because the rays are diverged away from the center line, there is less chance for overlap and confusion due to peripheral vision effects.

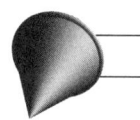

I INTRODUCTION TO 3-D VISUALIZATION

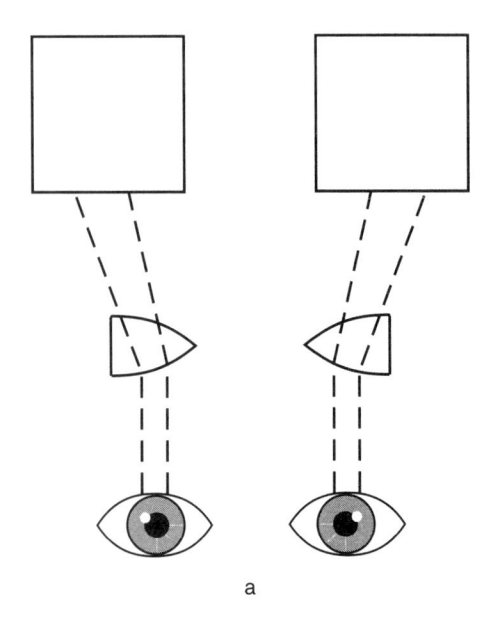

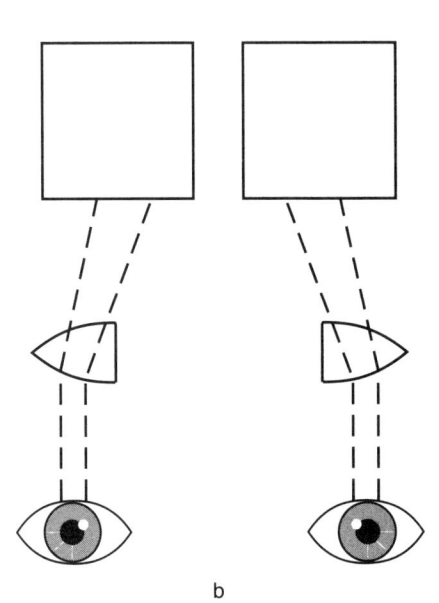

Figure 2.3

Half-lens viewing.

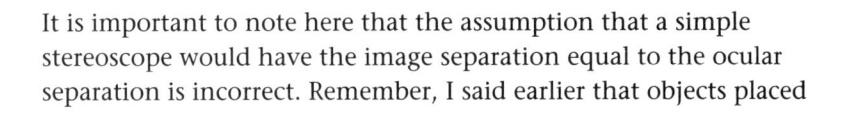

It is important to note here that the assumption that a simple stereoscope would have the image separation equal to the ocular separation is incorrect. Remember, I said earlier that objects placed

THE HISTORY OF 3-D IMAGING

at infinity are flat. If light follows a parallel path to the eyes, it is the same as light from an infinite distance (fig. 2.4), and therefore no 3-D effects are seen.

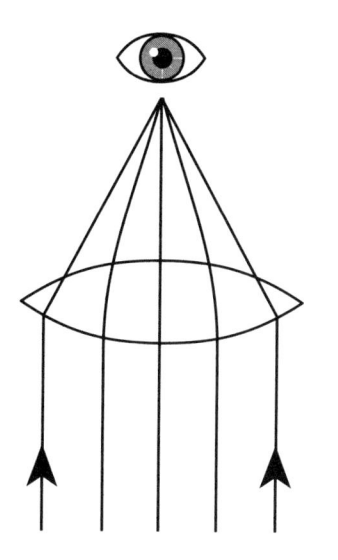

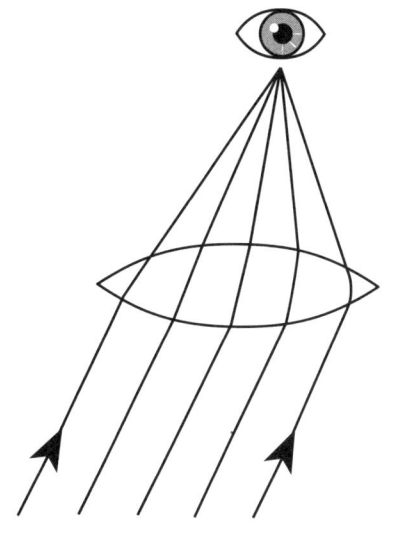

Figure 2.4

Parallel light through a positive lens.

Other variations such as making the eye separation wider or narrower cause the rays to diverge or converge, which makes for uncomfortable or difficult viewing. In both of these cases, the eyes must go out of line, which goes against the natural muscle control.

The Brewster Stereoscope is the earliest known lens stereoscope. In it, Sir David Brewster placed half-round lenses with the curved edges facing toward each other. Brewster also experimented with quarter lenses, half-ground lenses, and sometimes circular-ground lenses. Using more than half a lens is a waste if the viewing method shown in figure 2.3a is used, so to keep costs down, half-lenses became the norm for this type of device.

Figure 2.5 shows the Holmes stereoscope invented by famous American Oliver Wendell Holmes. Again, the half-lenses refract the light away from the central axis so that image clarity is preserved. The Holmes stereoscope was designed for use with the stereo cards that were popular around the latter part of the 19th century.

I INTRODUCTION TO 3-D VISUALIZATION

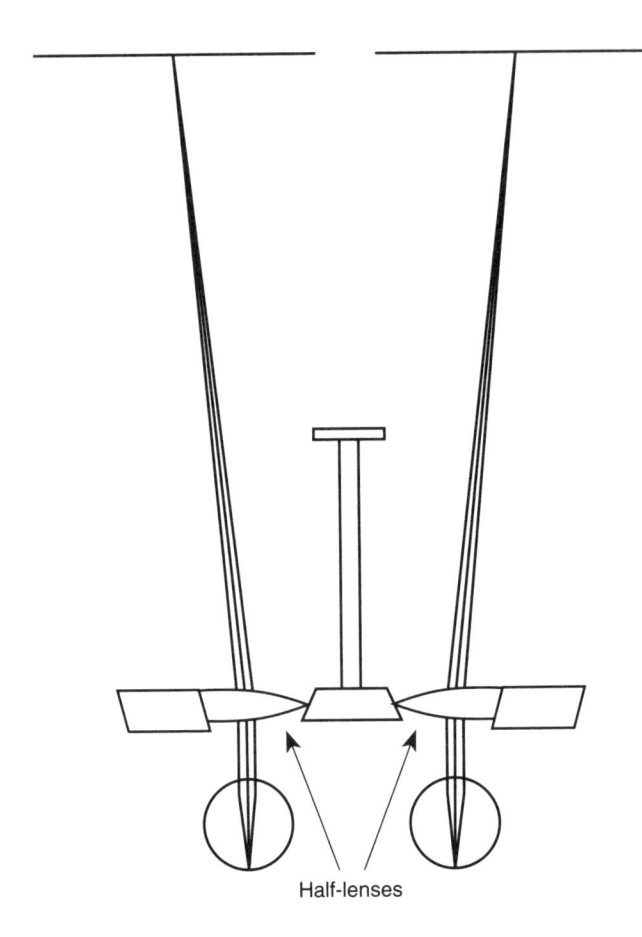

Figure 2.5

The Holmes reflecting stereoscope.

Half-lenses

Many other lens-based designs followed, but most were cheap attempts and gimmicks. The basics of the original stereoscopes are maintained even today.

Modern Reflecting Stereoscopes

The modern reflecting stereoscopes like the one in figure 2.6 overcome Wheatstone's image reversal problem by using two mirrors. Light is reflected from the large mirror surface to the small mirror surface, then on to the eye. These contemporary devices can be adjusted much like binoculars for viewing images up to poster size.

Sometimes lenses are added for magnification, but most are sealed with plastic covers only to keep out dust and small optical-impairing debris. Other variations include a reflecting stereoscope mounted on collapsible legs for adjusting its viewing height to accommodate various image sizes. The Wild ST4 Mirror Stereoscope is such a device. The best use for this device is when viewing color plates in a large-format book. The book can be opened up and laid flat on a table with the stereoscope propped up above it. The viewer then looks straight down through the device.

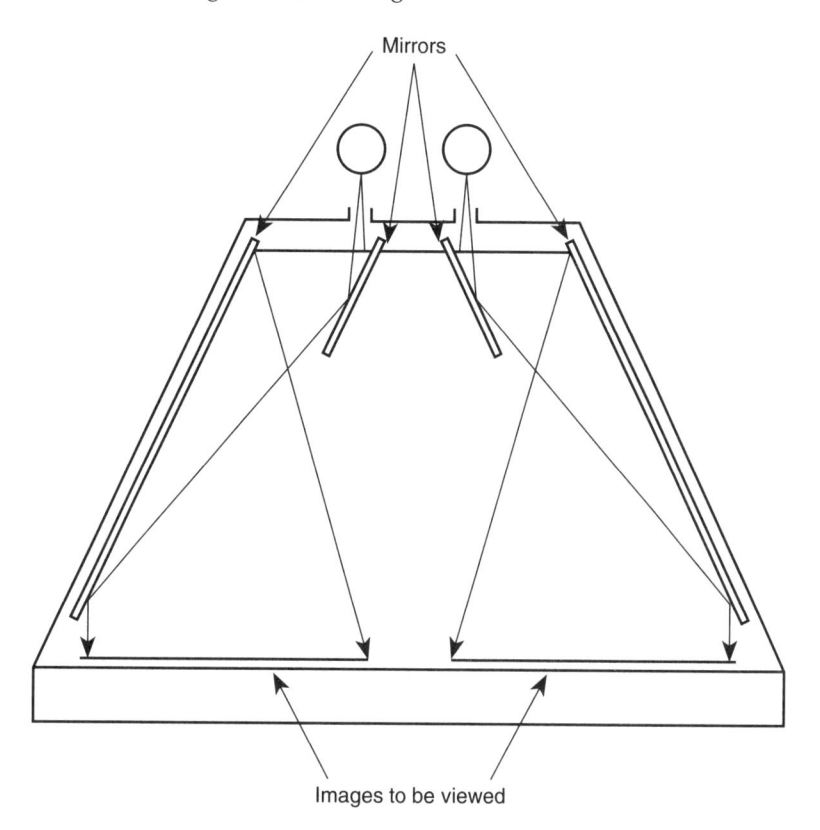

Figure 2.6

A modern reflecting stereoscope.

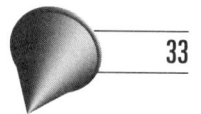

In all stereo viewing devices, it is preferable to keep the use of lenses to a minimum. There are two main reasons for this. First of all, optical impurities mean that light gets refracted in many different directions. And when you're trying to resolve minute differences between images, every photon counts! The second is that it is a property of optics that all glass lenses reflect some light as well as refracting it. Even the clearest glass will reflect away important light which is used for stereo discernment. In addition, some of the reflected light often comes back to the eye, further confusing the image.

The Kaiser Panorama

Another stereoscopic viewing invention in the late part of the 19th century was the Kaiser Panorama. It is not known exactly who invented this device, but credit usually goes to A. Fuhrmann, whose company Welt-Panorama Zentrale owned and operated these devices all over Germany and throughout central Europe.

The device was a large, cylindrical shell with 18 to 24 simultaneous stereo viewing devices spread around its circumference. Viewers sat around the outside of this device and an operator rotated the images inside so that after a short sitting, the viewer had seen 40 to 50 images. This might very well be the first rendition of the modern movie theater! People would come from miles around just to see a series of stereo images.

Welt-Panorama used only the best professional photographers and thus gained a reputation for providing the best quality images. Even today, several thousand of the original images are preserved in museums in Europe and are still regarded as some of the finest ever created. Performances are still given today at one remaining Panorama owned by the Berliner Festspiele GmbH in Berlin. This particular unit dates back to 1885, and is a splendid mahogany-paneled work of art.

Early 3-D Photographs and Cameras

Photography was invented in 1839. Although it is believed that the first cameras were purely mono, the idea of the stereo camera came soon afterward. In 1847, Sir David Brewster presented a paper in which he suggested ideas for a stereo camera. Although there is no definitive proof that this was the first stereo camera, it is generally believed to be true. In 1856, the London Stereoscopic Company published a catalog of stereo cameras following Brewster's designs. By 1860, taking stereo photographs and viewing the images was popular.

This led to a very interesting occurrence. In the late 1800s and early 1900s, there was no television. There were no movie theaters. Travel, especially international travel, was reserved for the wealthy. Newspapers reported only local news. All recording media of the day were flat or immobile. Paintings were a popular way to see the views of other cultures, but they were 2-D. Statues were so big and heavy that they didn't move around much.

Enter stereo photography. Suddenly, it became the entertainment medium of the turn of the century. A format was developed as a pseudo-standard (the stereo cards mentioned earlier in conjunction with the Holmes Reflecting Stereoscope). Now you could see the world, its art, its culture, and its architecture without ever leaving your house. You could trade cards with your friends. And all in 3-D.

This enthusiasm lasted well into the 20th century, until it was finally supplanted by motion pictures. Movies in 3-D also made a brief showing, but the difficulty was in shooting the movie (twice the film was necessary) and in developing a comfortable viewing environment for a hundred or more people. Today, these stereo cards are available in antique shops all over and can be quite valuable, depending on the photographer and the subject.

Although I have only touched briefly on the subject, by now you may be wondering why stereo photography isn't a bigger topic today. If it can generate all this hype and emotion, why has it never gone much beyond a fun hobby? There are two main reasons.

The first and most obvious reason is that it remains a still photography format. The emotions generated by major motion pictures far surpass those evoked by any 3-D photo that could be taken. The second lies in the technology itself. I won't go into it in great detail, because it is beyond the scope of this book, but to properly mount a stereo pair for decent viewing takes a great deal of skill. Many factors contribute to the quality of a stereo pair. The way the photo was taken, the way the film was processed and cropped during development, and the solidity of the viewing device all have a great effect.

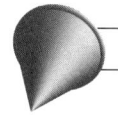

The "standard" card format solved some of these problems; however, the problems with cameras and stereo photography in general are numerous. For example, I spoke earlier of accommodation and convergence. Our eyes do this naturally. A camera does not. A good stereo photographer must know how to properly gauge convergence and adjust the cameras to compensate for the lack of muscular action human eyes have. The evolution of the motion picture came so quickly that the development of stereo photography as an industry was left to amateurs and those few professionals who did it for love rather than money.

Viewmaster

The most popular mass-marketed stereo picture format in the United States is Viewmaster, invented by Wilhelm Gruber in 1938. The Viewmaster format is unique in that, at 10.5×11.7 millimeters, it is the smallest commercial format available. It also became a big commercial success because of the availability of its standard viewing reels. A Viewmaster reel holds seven stereo pairs mounted at opposite sides of a circular cardboard frame (see fig. 2.7).

A great number of classic art reels were created, and there have been four different Viewmaster cameras to date. Three used 35mm film that was divided into an upper and lower row of frames. A fourth camera used 16mm film.

The other contribution of Viewmaster is the inexpensive plastic viewer. Most of us born in the latter half of the 20th century had numerous Viewmaster cartoon film reels as children. It also turned out that a predefined format for which specific cameras were created helped to provide a great deal of quality control over the images and the mountings.

Viewmaster reels are known for their technical workmanship. Taking large amounts of Viewmaster pictures is easy and cheap thanks to the adaptation of 35mm film to the task. For the budding amateur 3-D photographer, this is the preferred method of getting acquainted with the subject. The last cameras were made in 1972, though, so getting good equipment depends on finding a high-quality used camera shop.

THE HISTORY OF 3-D IMAGING

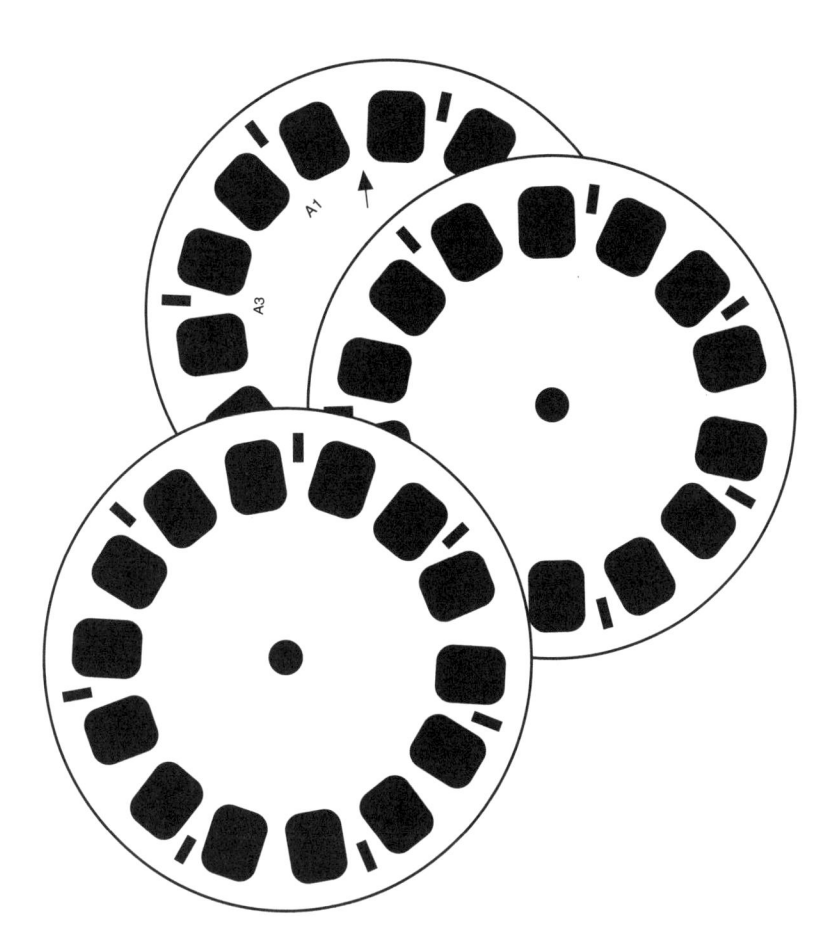

Figure 2.7

Viewmaster reels.

Modern Stereo Cameras

The term "modern" hardly applies to stereo cameras and equipment. The big boom of stereo cameras in the 1950s has died off to almost nothing. In fact, the last ones manufactured were released in the late 1960s and early 1970s.

Without standards, the problem of accurate mounting rears its ugly head. Many hobbyists have found methods of attaching two normal 35mm cameras together. This has the advantage of using normal 35mm film to create stereo slide pairs.

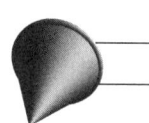

There are also devices such as the slide bar that mounts to a tripod. The camera is attached at one end of a metal, grooved bar. One photograph is taken, then the camera is slid to the other end for the other picture. This format has the distinct disadvantage that the subject cannot move between shots. For this type of shot (non-moving subject) the *Erskine shift* technique is easiest. Named after Dr. Stephen Erskine, a stereo hobbyist in rural England, this maneuver is accomplished by putting all the weight on one leg, taking a picture, then shifting the weight to the other leg to take the second. Although it sounds inaccurate, incredible results can be obtained.

Nimslo Lenticular Photography

In the early 1980s, Jerry Nims and Allen Lo created a camera and procedure for taking pictures that could be viewed in 3-D without the aid of a special viewing device. The method for creating these images had been around for some time, but the camera was a novel idea for amateurs. Previously, lenticular images required many sources, whereas the Nimslo camera required only four.

A lenticular 3-D picture has a thick, refracting, plastic coating on it so that if you move it under the light, the 3-D images appear (see fig. 2.8). Many baseball trading cards of the late 1970s used a similar technique. To generate a lenticular stereogram requires the use of multiple source images, rather than the normal pair. This is because a lenticular grid is a series of convex "bumps" in the plastic coating. Each source image gets refracted into an image line. By adjusting the separations from each of the source images, a band of image lines is created. Because each of these lines gets refracted back out to the eye during viewing, it appears to the viewer that the images are at different depths, thus creating the illusion that real-world viewing is taking place.

THE HISTORY OF 3-D IMAGING

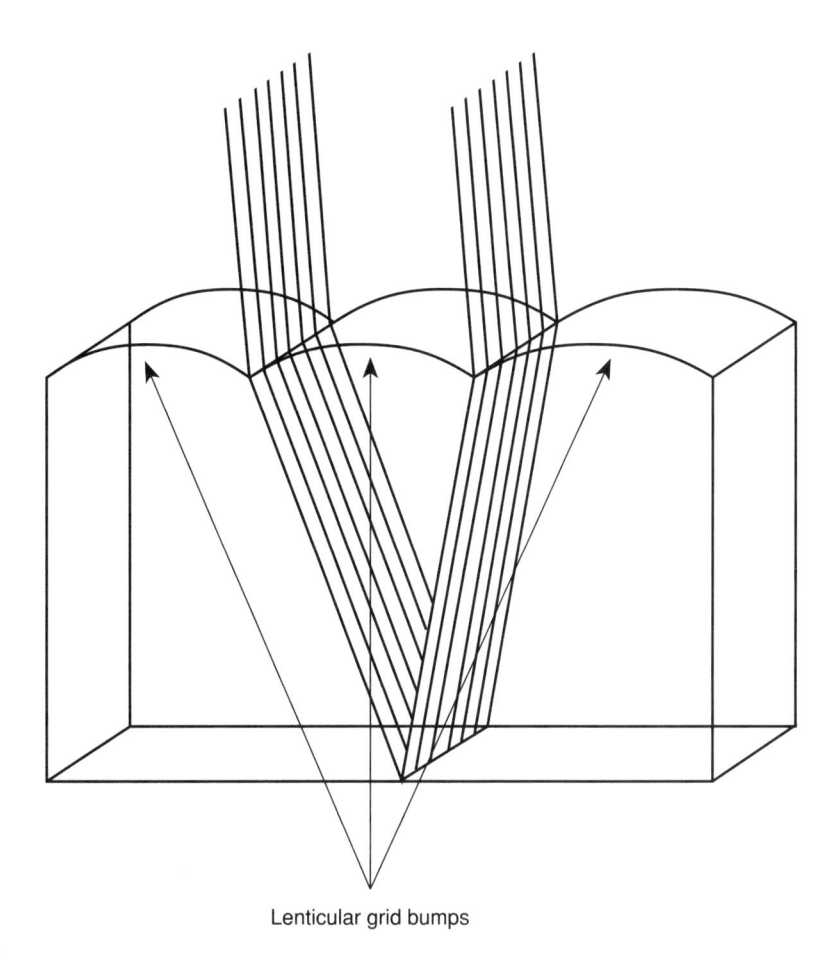

Lenticular grid bumps

Figure 2.8
Lenticular optics.

Summary

Stereo photography and viewing have been around for more than 150 years. Surprisingly, its popularity rises and falls, but it has never really emerged as a professional discipline. Consumer products such as the Viewmaster system have helped perpetuate the art; however, a lack of standards and quality control during preparation for display has kept stereo photos in the hobbyist realm. There are current consumer products such as the Nimslo four-image camera for simple work and classic used stereo cameras for higher-end investigation of the subject. When Wheatstone and Brewster invented stereo viewing and photography, they had no idea how big an impact it would have on their children's generation. I wonder what they would they would say if they knew about the coming onslaught of computers in the 3-D image world. You'll get a first glimpse in the next chapter.

3-D Images and Viewing Techniques

Stereo Pairs

I have discussed stereo pairs and stereoscopes briefly in previous chapters, but now it is time to get down to business. Even with the correct equipment, stereo viewing is a difficult task. Around the turn of the century, when stereo viewing as a hobby was at an all-time high, individuals prided themselves in their ability to properly gain the 3-D effect of the image they were viewing. The quality of the "3-Dness" is equally dependent on the accuracy of the mounting of the pair of images and the viewer's ability to alter his normal sight procedures in order to resolve 3-D.

Relaxed Stereo Viewing

Earlier, I discussed the contribution of convergence to creating a cyclopean image in our brains. To summarize, each eye focuses on the same point from a slightly different position. Because depth exists in the real world, objects in view lie at different distances from the eyes, and these images are superimposed naturally.

However, a photograph is a *planar*, or 2-D, image. Therefore, all objects in the image lie at the same physical distance from the eyes, so stereo effects are not possible. The fundamental premise of stereo pair viewing is to somehow allow each eye to see only the image it was intended to see, duplicating real-world viewing.

The simplest form of this is parallel viewing (see fig. 3.1a). In parallel viewing, each eye looks straight ahead and can see only the appropriate image. This philosophy has some problems, however. The most obvious is that the center of the images must be separated by the same distance as the eyes, or the problem of divergence arises (see fig. 3.1b). This means that the images must be rather small, which makes it difficult for them to be interesting.

Figure 3.1

Parallel viewing and divergence.

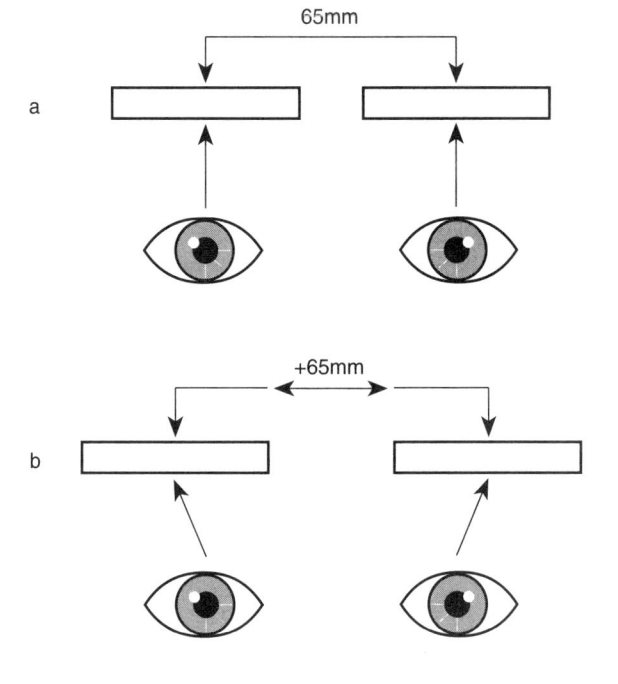

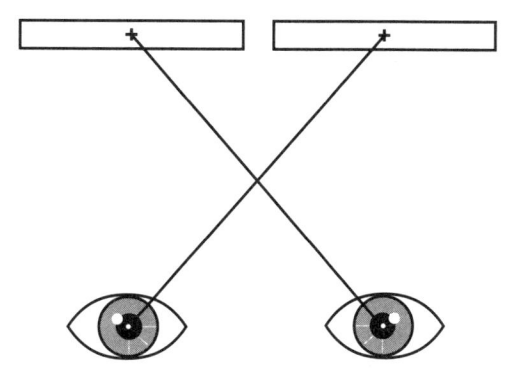

3-D IMAGES AND VIEWING TECHNIQUES

Figure 3.2
Cross-eyed stereo viewing.

Many stereo images are taken with cameras using normal 35mm film. These pairs are obviously too far separated to view in a parallel manner. Commercial applications such as medical x-rays or MRI photographs are also too large a format to view with parallel viewing.

As children, we learned how to make a funny face by looking down our noses until our eyes became crossed and our friends laughed. Making our eyes converge toward each other in this extreme manner is a relatively simple task for most humans. The converse is not true, however. Making the eyes diverge is a complicated and uncomfortable task, and if viewing stereo pairs depended on it, the hobby would be spoiled. Interestingly enough, though, we can apply the theory suggested in figure 3.1b if we resort to an old childhood trick.

Instead of forcing our eyes to diverge, we simply reverse the position of the images and view them cross-eyed (see fig. 3.2). These two methods require some practice, but are possible without the aid of a viewing device. For practice, let's use the stereo drawing (fig. 3.3) devised by Wheatstone in 1838 to illustrate his new invention, the stereoscope.

Bring the page close to your eyes. Relax your eyes by looking at the spot between the images as though you could see through the paper and across the room. Do not focus on each image individually. What you should see after some relaxation of the eyes is a three-image picture. After the center image appears, you find that you can "focus" on it. You aren't really focusing on it, of course, because it doesn't really exist. It is foremost in your brain, however, and you *believe* you can see it. This is an example of relaxed, unassisted

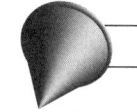

I INTRODUCTION TO 3-D VISUALIZATION

stereo viewing with the *parallel* method. If properly executed, you should see a "cone" receding into the page.

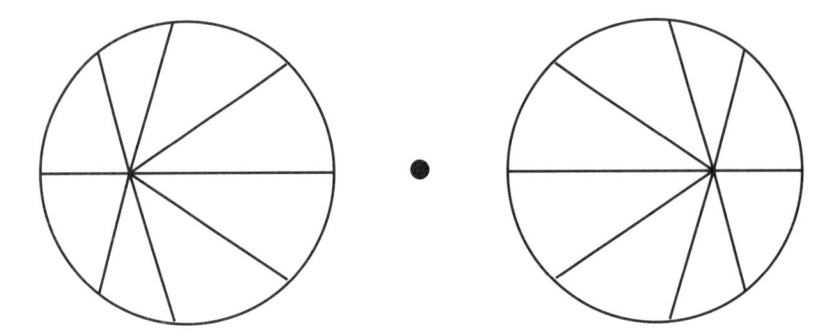

Figure 3.3

Wheatstone's stereo drawing.

The other method of relaxed stereo viewing is executed by looking down your nose until you are looking cross-eyed at the page. The same phantom third image will appear, but this time (unless you have turned the book upside-down) the cone appears to be protruding out of the book toward your face. Most people find this method much easier than parallel viewing because the nose is used as a gimmick to help relax the eyes and other portions of the viewing anatomy.

In both parallel and cross-eyed relaxed viewing, we generate a 3-D image from two 2-D images. A side effect of this technique is the creation of distortion, which makes it appear as if perspective exists.

In figure 3.4a, you see the results of this effect. The inside edge of each image appears to be receding into the page. In fact, the images are so close to your eyes that the inside edge is closer than the outside edge, thus introducing a new problem. However, our eyes are so good at compensating for such disturbances that in most cases we hardly notice. If you do notice and find the viewing uncomfortable, try slightly elevating the outside edge of each image so that it remains "flat" against your eyes (see fig. 3.4b).

Whether using parallel or cross-eyed stereo viewing, most individuals find the procedure to be strained and uncomfortable. It is an acceptable method for hobbyists who are trying for quick resolution to test a mounted pair, but for commercial or fun viewing, it proves too strenuous. For this reason, we turn to a multitude of stereo viewing products.

3-D IMAGES AND VIEWING TECHNIQUES

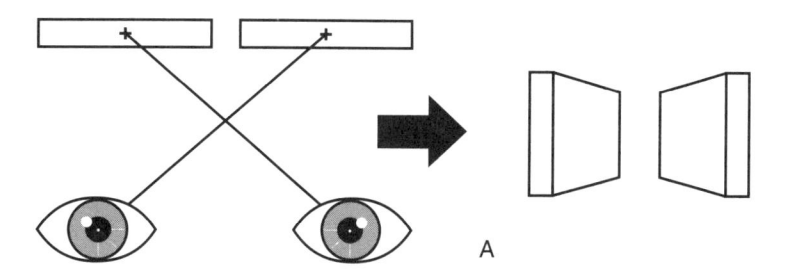

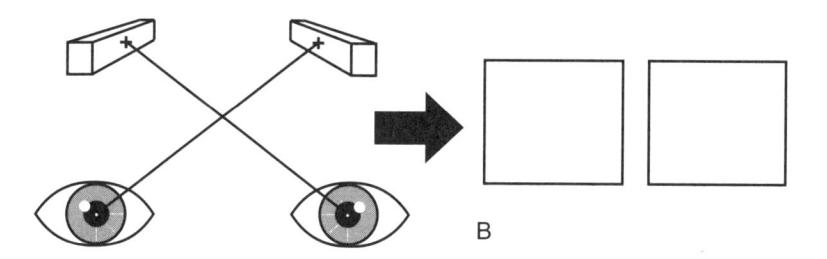

Figure 3.4

Perspective distortion.

Stereoscopic Viewers

The simplest type of mechanical assistant for stereo viewing is the hand-held lens stereoscope. This device uses half-circle portholes (much like Brewster's lens stereoscope) that keep the optic cones from crossing and help keep the line of sight for each eye directed toward its respective image. When combined with a slightly convex lens, it provides the ability to view stereo pairs with larger than 65mm separation. It has a slightly curved handle that drops below the axis of the lenses so that it is easy to hold in the hand without having the arm and fingers interfere with the viewing. Although simple and inexpensive, it allows the viewing of most standard stereo pairs. The device is held between the eyes and the image (see fig. 3.5). The distance between the eyes, lens, and image is adjusted manually until proper resolution is achieved.

This method is quick and inexpensive, and has quite good results in most cases. The primary drawback of this type of device is that because it is inexpensive, the lenses (usually plastic) are of poor optic quality and the clarity of the images often suffers as a result.

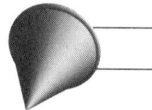

Figure 3.5

A hand-held lens stereoscope.

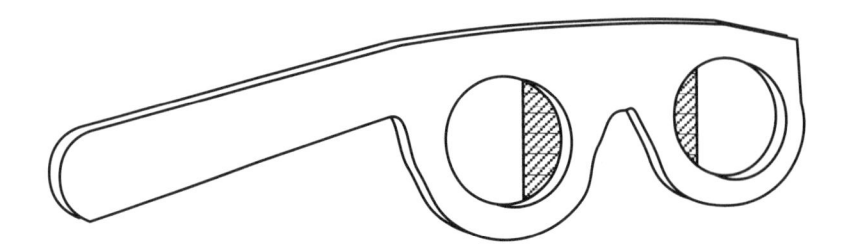

A variation of the hand-held lens stereoscope is the self-standing lens stereoscope. It works on the same principle as the hand-held stereoscope; however, because the distance to the image is fixed, the device is best-suited for viewing images of a fixed size. As a result, these images are much more easily resolved. All of the stereo pairs in this book can be viewed with this device.

Unlike the hand-held device, the standing stereo viewer has a partition which separates the optic cones and thus, the images. This aids in easy viewing and clear separation. The distance between the eye and the lens is adjusted for focus and clarity. Although this distance can be varied, it has rather severe limits, and its usefulness beyond simple stereo pair viewing is questionable. To use a self-standing lens stereoscope, unfold it into the position shown in figure 3.6. Place the stereoscope directly on top of an image and look down through the lenses.

The next step up the stereoscope ladder is the reflecting stereoscope. The lucky stereo hobbyist will find an original Holmes Stereoscope at an antique shop, along with a collection of classic stereo pairs. The Holmes model still provides entertainment, but works only with images specifically created for it. Although all designs relate back to the original Wheatstone model, the adjustable reflecting stereoscope by VCH is one of the easiest to use. The sides flex in and out much like binoculars to fit the viewer's eyes. With this stereoscope, images as large as posters can be viewed effortlessly. In fact, the VCH comes with a free stereo poster which confirms this capability. The hand-held, standing and reflecting stereoscopes are available through Reel 3-D Enterprises. See Appendix A for details.

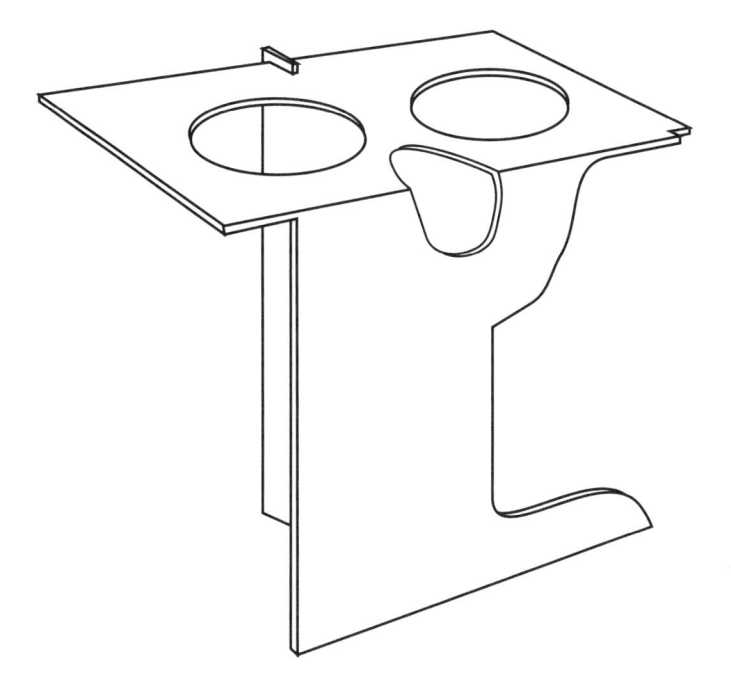

Figure 3.6

A standing lens stereoscope.

Random-Dot Stereograms

Bela Julesz was a pioneer in the field of cyclopean imagery. His random-dot stereograms proved conclusively that we had binocular vision by eliminating all monocular cues in an image.

You will remember that earlier you saw how certain factors such as lighting, shading, and reflections helped even a vision-impaired person to perceive three dimensions. A random-dot stereogram looks much like a random pattern of dots on a page. But when resolved into 3-D, a cyclopean image emerges. A sample random-dot stereogram is in figure 3.7. See if you can see the hidden shape in the image using the relaxed-eye method.

Random-dot stereograms offer a useful method for sending encrypted messages. If a message is sent as a random-dot stereogram, one image at a time, there is absolutely no way to decipher the message without having access to both images. As long as different routes are used to transmit the images, it is fairly secure. It is probably not acceptable for national defense issues, but it's a lot of fun for hobbyists.

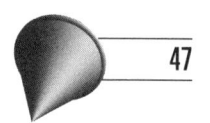

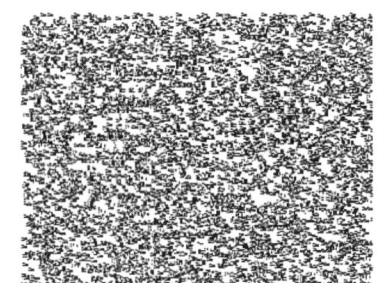

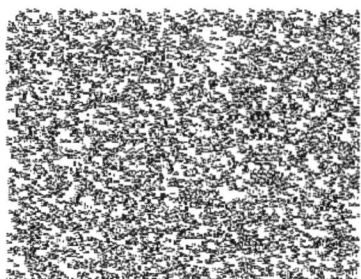

Figure 3.7

Julesz' random-dot stereogram.

A company called NE Thing Enterprises distributes single-image, random-dot stereograms. These special images have a built-in viewing system. By staring at a dot in the top center of the image, you see a stereo effect. The dot is an aid in relaxed stereo viewing. For more information, see Appendix A.

Anaglyph Imagery

We have illustrated repeatedly that the way to reconstruct stereo imagery is by isolating the left- and right-eye images through the viewing apparatus. Sometimes, it is useful to alleviate the requirement of having two separate images as source material. The single-image, random-dot stereograms of the previous section are an example of such an image. But it is impossible to take real-world photography and generate the same results through SIRDS. This problem has led to the development of many different techniques, the most popular of which is anaglyph imagery.

An anaglyph image is created by taking the source images (from a stereo pair) and tinting them each a different color. Then, when the images are viewed through complimentarily colored spectacles, each eye receives only information from that complimentarily colored image. In other words, if the left image is tinted blue and the right image is tinted red, a pair of glasses with a red filter on the left lens and a blue filter on the right lens will mask off those colors, allowing only the complimentary colors to pass through. When this happens, the left eye sees only the left image and the right eye sees only the right image.

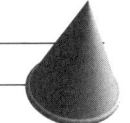

3-D IMAGES AND VIEWING TECHNIQUES

Anaglyph images come from many sources. Several good comic books have been published in anaglyph mode, namely those by Ray Zone in San Diego, CA. Comics in 3-D are specifically drawn that way, whereas anaglyph photography most often begins with black-and-white images. The separate images are filtered and combined to produce the anaglyph effect.

The biggest drawback to anaglyph images is that because they must be so heavily tinted red and blue, the color content of the result is limited. Also, because no color filter is perfect, a ghosting effect is created when either of the colors passes through the wrong lens. This ghosting can also be created when there are large amounts of overlapping image portions which are separated in the real-world source.

Anaglyph imagery also has many applications in the large-format fields such as x-ray and other medical uses. With anaglyph imagery, some of the problems spoken of earlier in viewing large stereo pairs are overcome.

In Europe, green and red are the preferred colors for anaglyph viewing. It is not known exactly why this is the preference. Certainly in the U.S., the preference is toward red and blue or red and cyan. Because red and blue are farther away in light frequency on the color spectrum, it makes sense that a better job of filtering can be done. Recently, a move has been made toward red and cyan.

It is commonly felt that by leaving some of the green in the blue image, better color preservation occurs when making an anaglyph from a color stereo pair. Although the result is still heavily red and blue, some components of red, green, and blue are present in the result image, thus allowing portions of the in-between colors to pass through. In Chapter 6, we look further into anaglyph imagery and put to use the red/blue glasses included in this book.

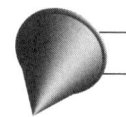

Anaglyphs also prove to be the simplest form of 3-D image to project for large audience viewing. I have already shown that stereo viewing depends heavily on proper alignment and image distances, which makes it difficult to gain decent results in a theater setting. Other methods are less dependent on image size and placement and are suited nicely to large audiences. Along with anaglyphs, these include polarized images and alternating shutter-glasses. Among these three, anaglyph is the easiest to create and the least expensive to view in terms of additional hardware or custom spectacles requirement.

Polarized 3-D Images

To understand how polarized 3-D image viewing is possible, a basic knowledge of optics is necessary. When light travels from one place to another, it is called *propagation*. Light rays travel only in a straight line. The direction the light travels is called the *direction of propagation*. As a light ray travels, it is constantly pulsating. This pulsation is the light ray's wave form and has amplitude and frequency like many other waves.

Sometimes light acts more like a particle than a wave. When it does, it can be studied as such. Scientists call this the *wave-particle duality of light*. Depending on which is more convenient for the application, they choose the appropriate model which best suits their needs. For our needs, we will stick with the wave analogy. The waves extend outward at right angles from the direction of propagation. They also extend in all directions around the direction of propagation (see fig. 3.8).

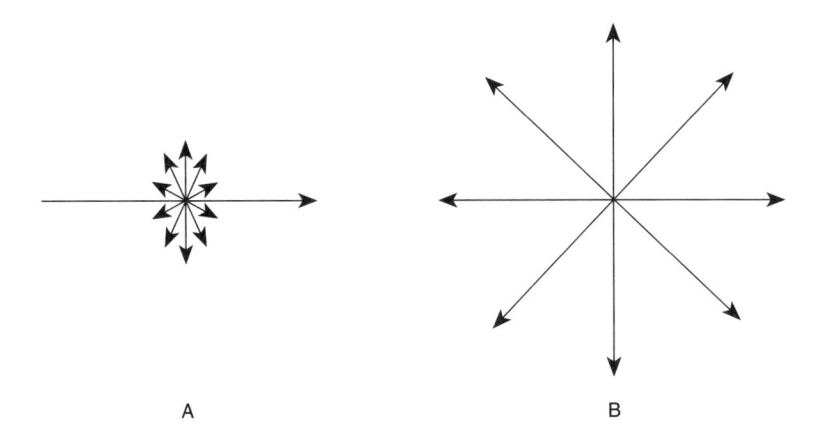

A   B

Figure 3.8

Light ray propagation.

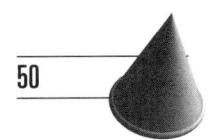

If you could see light coming straight at you, it would appear as in figure 3.8b. Light doesn't spin or rotate. What this means is that if you make a filter with a horizontal slit in it so that only the

3-D IMAGES AND VIEWING TECHNIQUES

horizontal waves pass through it, the waves will continue to be horizontal. They don't spin around the axis. When light has been filtered in this way, we say that it has been *polarized*. All polarized light has a direction of polarization associated with it.

As you can see from figure 3.9, if we put another filter, this time a vertical slit, in front of our horizontally polarized light, no light passes through. When using polarized light to work in optics, it usually takes two lenses. The first polarizes the light and the second operates on it.

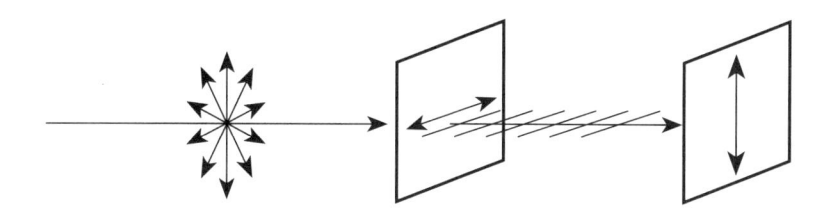

Figure 3.9

Polarization filtering.

If we extend this theory to 3-D images, or more specifically stereo pairs, we have a very convenient viewing mechanism. Using figures 3.8 and 3.9 for reference, we see that if we polarize the left image horizontally, a horizontal lens over the left eye allows only the light from that image to pass through. The same holds true for the right eye. If we use vertical polarization for the right eye, we avoid any possibility for overlap of the two images.

In practice, it has been found that diagonal polarization works best for polarized projection. This is because for horizontal-vertical polarization to work properly, the viewer's head must be kept perfectly horizontal. The diagonal polarization compensates for some of this. Also, unless it is a totally dark room, other light interferes and causes ghosting to occur.

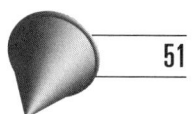

It turns out that for projection of 3-D, polarized techniques are the simplest and provide the best results. This is due in part to the fact that normal projection screens with silver metallic coatings reflect light without much loss in the polarization. To generate a stereo presentation, one needs only two projectors (one for each image, a polarizing filter for each projector, and polarizing glasses for the audience. The glasses are inexpensive and can be made from plastic without worry of image loss due to poor optics. There is some degree of image loss because not all of the projected light can pass through the polarizing filters; this is easily compensated for by turning up the intensity of the projectors.

Holographic Images

Another type of 3-D imagery which is beyond the scope of this book but bears mentioning is *holography*. A hologram is created by combining reflected monochromatic light with nonreflected light from the same source (see fig. 3.10). Monochromatic light means light that is all one color or frequency. Each different frequency of light creates a different color. When the differences between frequencies in the same beam of light are very small, the light is said to be monochromatic.

The most common form of monochromatic light is the helium-neon laser. You may have seen a HeNe laser in science class or at a museum. It is recognizable because of its deep red light. There are other types of lasers that are of different colors, but they are usually more expensive and difficult to obtain. For home laser projects, a 500mw HeNe laser costs about $200.

When the two monochromatic light paths are combined, there are differences in the phase of the light due to the reflection. In short, holography is the analysis of these differences, called *interference patterns*. It turns out that if these differences are recorded onto photographic film and developed, when the same source of monochromatic light is applied to the photo, an image of the object that was used for reflection appears.

This result is unique in two ways. The first is that it is true 3-D. If we were to walk around the image, we would see all portions of it that were illuminated by the source light originally. If this image is projected, it looks like the original object is there in space in front of us. Of course, it isn't, but under the proper conditions, it is extremely difficult to tell that it is not actually there. The other unique property of this special photo is that any small portion of it contains all the information for the entire photograph! This is hard to believe without support, but an in-depth understanding of why it occurs requires an extensive knowledge of physics and is beyond our scope.

3-D IMAGES AND VIEWING TECHNIQUES

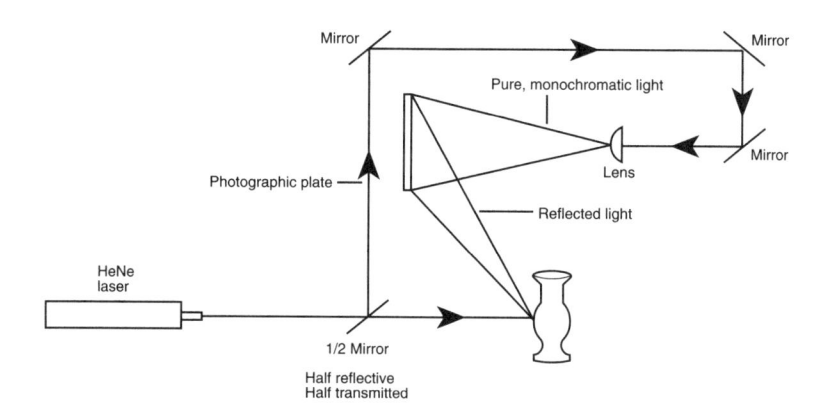

Figure 3.10

Holography.

Just imagine the possibilities if you could take a picture, then cut a little piece of the negative and reproduce the entire original picture. This technique finds applications in science, medicine, and document archival.

Holography has several problems which prohibit its use for common 3-D viewing. First of all, a holographic photographic setup requires special conditions. The room must be totally dark except for the laser light. No noise or other vibrations can exist. The air must be very clean. If you think about how small a light wave is (have you ever seen one?), you will understand how even the smallest particle of dust or smoke can have a great effect on the interference patterns generated.

Recently, commercial developers have invented ways of embedding holographic images into plastic in a way that enables them to be viewed under normal light. You may have seen such a hologram on your credit card. Although these images are called holograms, they are not the same as projecting a holographic image in its full 3-D splendor onto a laboratory table. The other problem with low-grade holography is that because the experiments are done with HeNe laser light, the results tend to be red in color. Special films help reduce this, but for the most part, red-tinted images are all that can be expected.

We are just learning to understand holography, and more will be written about it in the coming years. The wonders of holography are endless. If you are interested, check some of the references listed in Appendix A.

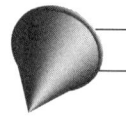

I   INTRODUCTION TO 3-D VISUALIZATION

The Pulfrich Effect

In the 1980s, several large corporations experimented with the use of 3-D in national commercials. These commercials were generated using the Pulfrich effect. To understand how this effect works, we must start with an understanding of light propagation.

Sound, as we all have learned, is subject to alterations in speed. Sound travels faster underwater than it does in air, for example. When a car is coming toward us, it sounds different than when it is going away. This difference is caused by a shift in the relative velocity of the sound waves. Light, however, travels at the same speed all the time (short of a discussion on special relativity, this is the commonly accepted position).

This speed is not measured relative to any other object. If you are inside the car mentioned previously, you do not hear the noise change because, relative to you, the car is not moving. Relative to a bystander on the side of the road, it is. Light, however, is the same. You both see the same colors and the same objects at the same time.

In the case of light, scientists have measured small shifts in its speed, but cannot explain them with the wave model of light. This is where the previously mentioned wave-particle duality of light comes in. The particle model does allow for an explanation, but we don't need to go into that here. The point of this discussion is that for our purposes, light always travels at the same speed. However, our eyes react differently to different intensities.

You might have noticed that it takes your eyes a little longer to focus in dim light than in bright light. This is the technique intrinsic in the Pulfrich effect. By covering one eye with a darkened lens, the light entering that eye is acknowledged by the brain slightly later than light which enters the uncovered eye.

Think about how animation on film works. Each frame of the film contains a successive image in the animation sequence. If an object is moving horizontally, it advances across the frame sequentially until it moves off the frame entirely (see fig. 3.11).

If we apply the Pulfrich effect by putting a dark lens over the left eye, the right eye sees one frame ahead of the left eye. Because the object has moved, the separation distance is interpreted by our

3-D IMAGES AND VIEWING TECHNIQUES

brains as a cyclopean image. If there are several images moving at different speeds, 3-D is created because the separation distance of the different objects is interpreted as a depth cue (see fig. 3.12).

Figure 3.11

Pulfrich effect animation.

Figure 3.12

Multiple objects and the Pulfrich effect.

As you have probably surmised by now, this type of film must be carefully generated. For example, if a slow-moving object is placed in front of the faster-moving object, we have a conflicting message in the brain. 3-D vision says that the faster-moving object is closer to us (greater separation distance), yet we "see" the slower object pass in front of the faster one (monocular cue). Also, if the objects move in the other direction, they will appear to recede into the screen instead of coming out of it toward the viewer. Vertical movements are not as easily recognized as being 3-D.

Video commercials advance at 30 frames per second. It turns out that this is fast enough to generate a good 3-D effect. However, it can be enhanced even further if a technique called *field framing* is used. Television signals are sent to us in interlaced fashion. That is, the horizontal lines across our screen are painted by the television in two passes (see fig. 3.13). If the successive images are changed 60 times per second rather than 30, they are more noticeable because the subtle changes in eye focusing and registration happen slowly enough to over-emphasize the effect.

Field framing has the side effect of making the commercial look fuzzy to those who are not wearing the special glasses, but this helps add to the hype of the commercial. Viewers feel they are missing something if they can't participate. If you study these commercials carefully, you will find that they are very carefully scripted to move from left to right (or whichever direction fits the

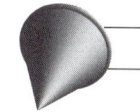

1 INTRODUCTION TO 3-D VISUALIZATION

glasses!) and employ simple, multiple-object motions. Although not true 3-D, it is an entertaining method for bringing 3-D to the masses via television.

Odd lines — Even lines

Figure 3.13

Interlaced images.

Recently, Coca-Cola ran a commercial on television using the field-framing technique. It was a cooperative venture with 7-11 convenience stores—a viewer had to visit a local 7-11 to get the glasses.

Summary

The world of 3-D images has many paths to follow. Each path has a slightly different toll, but most aren't too expensive. Stereo pairs and anaglyph images are the most common forms of 3-D viewing. Proper application of these techniques requires a stereoscope or "funny" red and blue glasses. For special applications, holography and the Pulfrich effect are useful. No matter which avenue you choose, the 3-D experience is one of unusual dimensions. With any luck, those dimensions will extend into the future and provide simulations like the "Holodeck" on "Star Trek: The Next Generation." In the next chapter, we investigate some current applications of 3-D technology.

3-D Visualization Applications

All the hype we can generate about 3-D would be of no value if there were no real-world application for it. Fortunately, this is not the case. Many established industries have learned to benefit from stereoscopic image analysis and stereo imaging in general. This chapter looks briefly at several of these applications, how they are implemented, and the benefits thereof. There are many other applications than are mentioned in this book, and I encourage you to investigate further if a particular topic of interest is not covered here.

Aerial Photogrammetry

One of the earliest and most obvious uses of stereophotography is in using aerial photographs for a variety of applications. Various surfaces of the Earth are beyond current capabilities of man to explore through conventional methods. Weather conditions and rugged terrain make climbing and mapping impossible.

I INTRODUCTION TO 3-D VISUALIZATION

Mount Everest was completely mapped in 3-D after a plane made a historic multiple-pass fly-by, taking stereo images along the way. The flight pattern resembled a grid when viewed from the air. Successive stereo photographs were taken as the plane flew along each gridline, then accurate terrain was mapped using a variation of the triangulation method of distance measurement. (*Triangulation* is the method where if the lengths of two sides of a triangle and an adjacent angle are known, the other length can be calculated.) Scientists discovered rock crags and ledges which were previously not accurately described. Many darkened areas that were previously thought to be just dark regions of rock were found to be shadows in places the sun never reached. Since that time, the technique has been used extensively for similar operations.

Another use for aerial photogrammetry is in the petrochemical industry. By carefully examining aerial photographs in 3-D, scientists can get a better understanding of large land formations. Certain types of formations indicate higher probabilities of oil and mineral content. 3-D analysis over large regions shows formations that are not discernible at ground level. Water basins, oil deposits, and fault lines are carefully analyzed using 3-D techniques.

An interesting mapping technique involves the use of anaglyph images rather than stereo. By taking high-resolution stereo photographs and combining them, very high-quality anaglyphs result. When scientists carefully overlay a small dot and move this dot along fused lines, a contour map emerges. This map can be very precise if the separation distance of the base (the distance between camera shots) is known and if the plane that took the images flew in a predictable pattern at consistent altitude.

Medicine

The medical field is probably the most advanced 3-D image user. Specifically, stereo microscopy enables doctors to get previously unavailable diagnostic information from within the human body. This makes the treatment of particular ailments possible with greater accuracy and with a higher level of confidence.

3-D VISUALIZATION APPLICATIONS

I have written a great deal about the eye so far. It is interesting that one of the best-known uses for 3-D imagery is in retinal analysis. A stereo picture is taken of the back of the eye, or retina. This is accomplished with a miniature version of a *beam splitter* (see fig. 4.1). A camera takes a picture from one angle, then a little electronically controlled prism alters the optic axis of the camera and a second picture is taken.

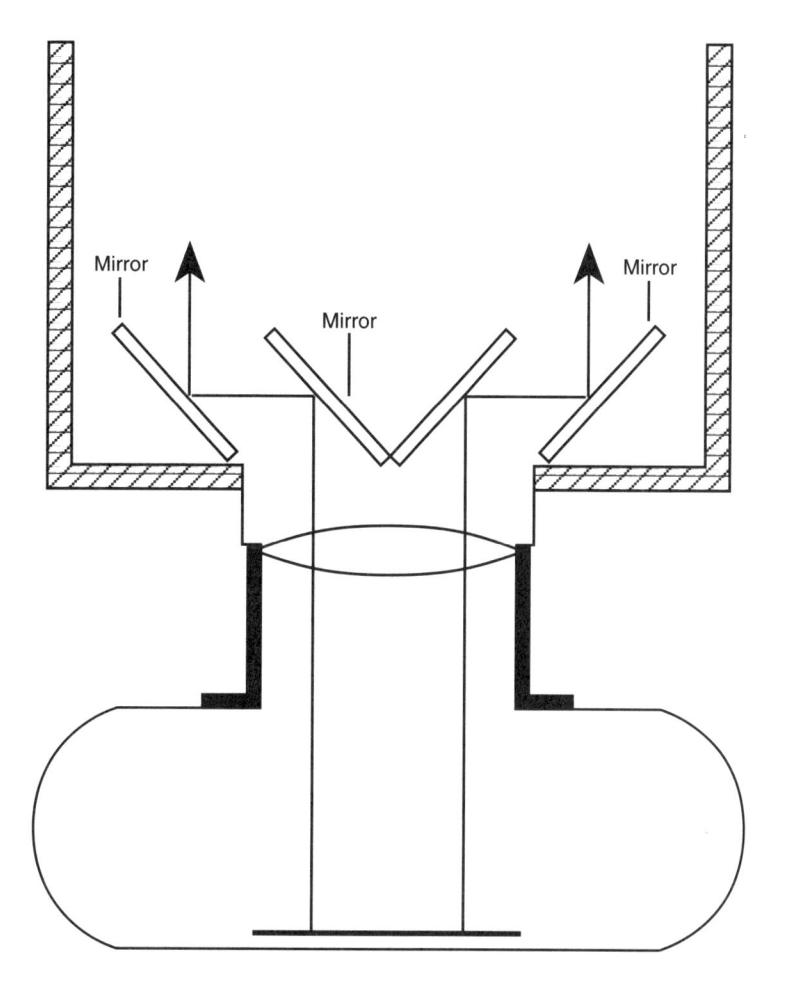

The two center mirrors can be replaced with a prism.

Figure 4.1

A beam splitter camera attachment.

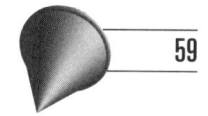

To most of us, the back of the eyeball would seem to be fairly consistent and uninteresting. In actuality, slight imperfections tell quite a bit about the condition of the patient. This is accomplished

I INTRODUCTION TO 3-D VISUALIZATION

by measuring the depth of the optic disk (the region of the eye where the optic nerve endings are implanted, also referred to as the *optic cup* due to its concave shape). If the optic cup is too concave, it might be an indication that the patient has too much pressure inside the eye, which suggests glaucoma. If the optic cup is flatter than expected, it could be an indication of cranial pressure due to a tumor or high blood pressure. This same technique is used for examining many different organs, bone structure, and the brain.

Much work is also being done in the area of 3-D sonograms, magnetic resonance imaging (MRI), and other scanning technologies. Scanning is the most contemporary method for looking at areas of the body without exploratory surgery. If this scanning is done in stereo, the results are more conclusive. If a 3-D MRI of the heart is created, the degree of curvature and thus internal pressure (much like the eye example) can be measured without having to take multiple images—or worse, perform surgery. A 3-D MRI animation can show exactly how a patient's heart is beating. Doctors use 3-D sonograms to analyze fetal development in pregnant women.

Specifically, a series of two-dimensional images are taken using a CAT-scan or MRI device. Then, using advanced computer graphics techniques, the images are combined to generate a 3-D video image. These images are useful for pre-operation planning. Using an electronic scalpel, the doctor can "practice" the operation before making an incision. For brain operations, this is incredibly useful, because the surgeon can accurately plan the incision path, avoiding contact with motor strips, which could cause paralysis.

This technique is also very important in major bone reconstruction. With the aid of the electronic image, a surgeon can plan how a bone should be cut and repositioned. Once this planning has taken place, a video print image can be used to actually mark positions on the patient's head for the incisions.

Not only has the medical profession used 3-D imaging to assist in planning, but it is starting to use it during operations as well. After the incision is made, a reference monitor is used to check progress. The video monitor acts as a picture book of the patient's internal organs, helping the surgeon avoid critical errors.

Architecture

The cost of lumber and other building materials is rising. Large residential tracts as well as major shopping centers need funding during development in order to maintain the building cycle. This used to be done by prebuilding models and suites to generate interest in prospective tenants and homeowners.

With the costs of building these "teaser" units so high, many architectural firms are turning to computer models to help sell the early units. It is much less expensive to take a set of plans, build a 3-D model, and "walk" through it than it is to build a real structure. Even the interior design can be put in with all the details, then changed on a whim. A designer can change carpets, repaint the walls, add furniture, and detail the kitchen. Using the non-cyclopean tricks of shadowing, reflections, and shading, very realistic renderings are generated. On a large screen or via videotape, these models are accurate enough and convey adequate emotion to persuade a purchaser to take the big step and put down a deposit.

Three-dimensional analysis also helps the structural engineer foresee potential problems. By applying force through mathematical models and applying the properties of the building materials to the equation, stress and fracture can be analyzed. Although this has been done for years through math and computer simulations, the modern ability to actually see it in 3-D greatly enhances the analysis process. Seeing a table of numbers that predicts how a building might sway in an earthquake and actually seeing it sway are two totally different things. Watching a landfill area settle and the house built on it crumble is far less damaging on a computer than in reality.

An architect is also able to generate views and see buildings from angles that are impossible in real life. The architect can fly through a crawl space, zip through electrical conduits, or travel the flow of a septic system—all from the computer console. Landscapes are created with computer-generated trees and shrubs. Long-term effects can be studied by growing the trees over time. Natural surroundings such as rocks and rolling hills can be added to the model. With the added element of 3-D, the information content of such travel through space and time is beyond compare.

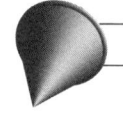

Military

Documentary photographers have been photographing military operations in 3-D for some time. As early as World War II, a variety of photographs on such subjects as barracks life and weaponry have emerged. One of the most famous 3-D war photographers is Bill C. Walton. His black and white stereo pairs chronicle everything from training to armored vehicle studies. Perhaps you have seen soldiers crawling on their bellies under low barbed wire in a war movie. Brought to life through the magic of 3-D, Walton's crawling soldier images breathe with emotion.

The military has long been one of the biggest users of aerial photogrammetry for reconnaissance and analysis of enemy territory. Camouflage techniques have improved over the years to fool even the most sophisticated surveillance methods. Shadows, shading, and terrain color matching make it difficult to spot a hidden tank, even when it's out in the open. But with stereo picture analysis, the shadows move relative to each other and send signals to the observer that an object of greater depth than previously observed may exist.

The military is also the world's greatest builder of bridges and dams. Stereo analysis of land masses provides much information to geological engineers. From accurate topographic mapping to mineral and chemical analysis, 3-D imagery plays a part in the process. The same structural and engineering applications that were mentioned in the section about architecture apply here as well. Knowing how a bridge will sway in the wind is valuable planning knowledge.

Entertainment

The entertainment business has tried 3-D on several occasions. From anaglyph movies to Pulfrich-effect shorts and commercials, producers have been trying to cash in on the hype that underlies 3-D viewing for many years. The first 3-D movie was generated in 1937 and was appropriately titled *Third-Dimension Murder*. It was anaglyph, of course, and therefore had to be a black-and-white film.

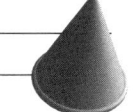

3-D VISUALIZATION APPLICATIONS

It wasn't until 1952 that the first color 3-D movie was released from Hollywood, *Bwana Devil*. This state-of-the-art film used the polarization technique. We often laugh when we see clips from the 50s of a theater full of moviegoers with silly looking glasses on their faces. The discomfort of the glasses and the lack of color after the anaglyph process made the appeal of these films limited.

However, color 3-D movies made a resurgence in the 1980s, when *Jaws III* and one of the *Friday the 13th* movies were shown in 3-D. During the summer of 1982, the movie *Return of the Creature* was shown on television in 3-D. In coordination with the event, 3-D glasses were sold at convenience stores; however, the movie was in black and white, and the red and blue "ghosting" was obvious.

In modern times, the Walt Disney Corporation shows a 3-D movie as part of the Disneyland experience, which uses polarized light and lenses for the effect. It is a modern sci-fi that is fast-paced and very dramatic. The effect is so strong that in one scene, a little alien creature appears to jump out of the screen and into the laps of the audience, amid shrieks and screams. The simple plastic framed glasses are lightweight and painless to wear. It is surprising that this type of film isn't more popular.

Across the park from the film is a 3-D ride that is spectacular. Although the 3-D effects are augmented with a movable seating platform, the video fly-through seems almost real as passengers grip their seat arms with white knuckles. The effect is so strong that pregnant women and those with heart conditions are asked not to ride!

On the home front, until recently, Sega made a 3-D game system based on 3-D LCD shutter technology. This technology is similar to the polarizing effect, except that only one image is displayed at a time and a very fast electronic LCD shutter alternately allows viewing through each eye, one at a time. When the left eye is open, the left eye image is shown, and the same is true for the right eye. This all happens at video speeds (30 times a second), so the viewer detects no flicker. These special lenses can be adapted to fit an IBM-compatible home computer.

A very interesting application in the entertainment world is the OmniMax theater. In OmniMax, you are surrounded with a spherical wall of moving image. The mere size of the image allows

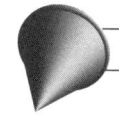

I INTRODUCTION TO 3-D VISUALIZATION

complete immersion into whatever world it is portraying. You can ride the rapids down the Grand Canyon, take a motorcycle around tight mountain roads, or fly at the speed of light through space without moving. It is not clear exactly why such a dramatic 3-D effect is generated, but it is probably due to the fact that your entire field of vision is filled with moving image. Without the sides of the screen as a point of reference, it is easy to relax and allow your brain to believe that you are really there.

Game technology has progressed along with computer technology to a point where we can now generate simple 3-D worlds in real time on a personal computer. This is the latest rage in computer gaming. Virtual worlds are created as data sets that the computer can draw from very quickly. The game player moves through this world at incredible speed, fighting and slashing through obstacles along the way. The freedom to play at any speed the player can handle adds a new dimension previously unavailable in computer games. From Pong to Pac-Man to other more modern games, the speed of the game was fixed by the computer. Now, a player plays as fast as he can. As technology increases, so will the graphics quality and performance of these games. New user interfaces such as helmets and gloves lead the way in gaming and simulation control devices. So much for the joystick!

Biology

One of the most common uses for stereo imagery among hobbyists is in photographing plants and wildlife. The study of nature is both entertaining and informative, and with 3-D it is realistic. Open virtually any book on 3-D and you will find closeup images of beetles, butterflies, flowers, and small mosses. There is so much to learn from looking around and under these subjects in ways that cannot be accomplished with 2-D. This hobby also requires the use of a special technique in 3-D photography called *macro stereoscopy*.

When dealing with close-ups, the separation of the lenses must be quite small. As a result, a hypo-stereo effect is generated. *Hypo-stereo* refers to a small lens separation which produces images that appear to be larger than expected. This is because when we view the pair

3-D VISUALIZATION APPLICATIONS

with our normal eye separation, the brain tells us that the objects in the scene are to be magnified by the same amount as the lens separation to eye separation ratio (see fig. 4.2).

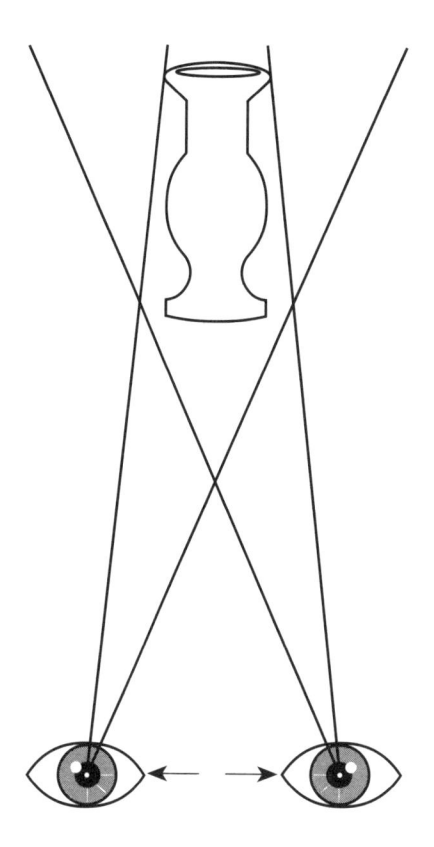

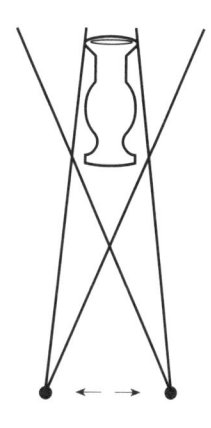

Figure 4.2

Hypo-stereo magnification.

Sometimes, this effect is useful. For example, hypo-stereo allows us to see further "under" an object than in normal stereo. It also happens to be one of the only ways to take 3-D pictures of small things. Insects and other biological specimens frequently fall into this category. Microscopic stereo images are obtained with only one microscope, but by tilting the subject plate slightly between exposures. If done very carefully, this simulates the effect of having the subject remain stationary and having two cameras (see fig. 4.3).

The study of microbes and subatomic particles in 3-D requires this technique. When dealing in subjects that are too small to see with the naked eye, 3-D must be generated through techniques such as

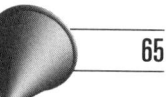

I INTRODUCTION TO 3-D VISUALIZATION

stereo microscopy, or else they would never be visible. With hypo-stereo, we are able to generate 3-D views and see how particles react to each other rather than just theorizing on the subject with mathematics and a few still photographs.

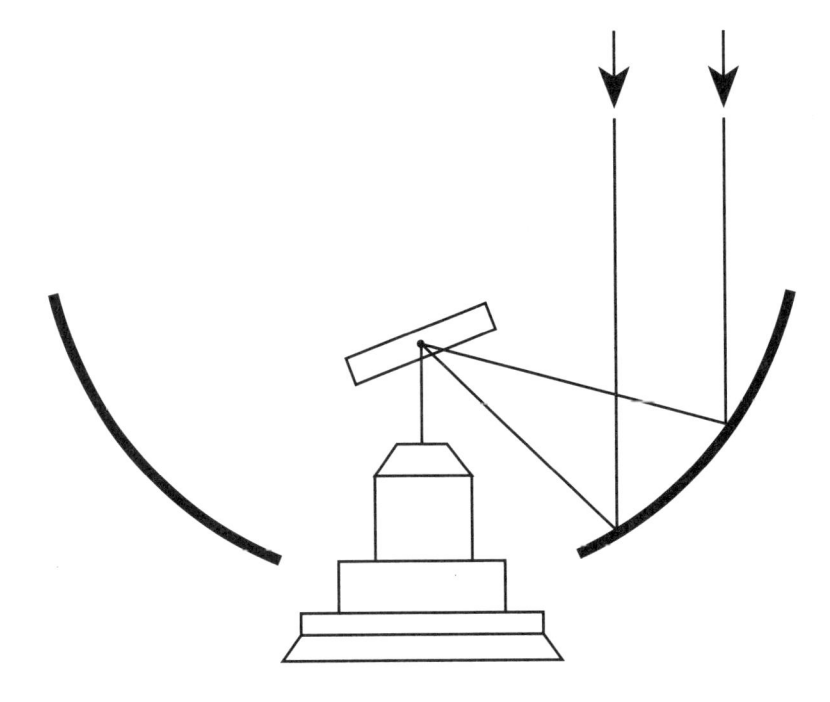

Figure 4.3

Tilting-plate microscopy.

Space

Since the earliest space missions, NASA has generated stereo pairs of its lunar missions. These images are available to the public and are free of charge. They include images of the first step on the moon and the famous golf swing in near-zero gravity.

More recently, NASA has generated stereo images of the fly-bys of Jupiter and Neptune. It is relatively simple to take a stereo pair during this type of maneuver, because the movement of the spaceship over time acts as a displacement device for the camera. By combining adjacent pairs in a series of photographs, 3-D animation can be created as well. This type of study is very important for measuring the depth of craters and other surface anomalies on distant planets.

3-D VISUALIZATION APPLICATIONS

Entire planet surfaces can be mapped by applying stereo photogrammetry techniques. Until we can generate enough energy to visit these faraway places in person, this is the only way to get a really good look at them. Telescopes can be used for stereo recording; however, the distance to the planets along with atmospheric problems make the resulting images imprecise. A spaceship flying by at only a few miles above the surface can gather crystal-clear images.

It is also possible to generate stereo pairs with a radio telescope. Radio waves can be collected and analyzed in much the same way as light waves. The primary difference is that the wavelength is longer, so the margin for error is greater. This is useful for measuring the size of gaseous objects such as comet tails and distant nebulae. Although the precision of these measurements is questionable, it can be argued that some measurement is better than no measurement at all!

Summary

Stereo pairs, anaglyphs, and monocular 3-D images are of great use to a wide variety of industries. With them, these industries can see, analyze, and measure components of their fields as never before. Advances in microscopes, telescopes, and computer processing contribute to this newfound success. As these technologies continue to improve our view of our world, we will learn things that until now were only dreams. And isn't it better to dream in 3-D? But look for most of these dreams to come to you via the entertainment industry. New technology requires a huge influx of cash; traditionally, the entertainment industry has been very reliable in that respect. 3-D programs are used everyday in the creation of movies and video games. In the next chapter, you take a look at current technologies and learn the fundamentals of how these programs work.

Part II

Using the Computer for 3-D Visualization

3-D Programs and Illusion Techniques

There is a big problem with trying to view 3-D images on a computer screen: the screen is a two-dimensional device! There is no way to get real-world depth on a two-dimensional device, because a true cyclopean image cannot be generated. There are techniques for dealing with dual-image viewing (namely stereo pairs), anaglyphs, and hardware screen flipping devices, which are covered later. This chapter focuses on how to use a computer to simulate three dimensions through the use of monocular cues.

You will remember from Chapter 1 that monocular cues are things such as perspective, shadows, highlights, and shading. There are also environmental conditions such as haze and fog which contribute to the three-dimensional effect of a 2-D image. In this chapter, we go through each of the contributing factors and examine techniques for generating the effects on a computer. We also look at particular types of computer programs that generate 3-D worlds with minimum effort. These programs are called 3-D modelers and renderers.

II USING THE COMPUTER FOR 3-D VISUALIZATION

Translating 3-D into 2-D

Before you look at effects due to lighting, it is important to examine the shape of objects seen on a computer screen. Chapter 3 dealt briefly with perspective, but here's a closer look. Exactly what is perspective and how does one generate it on a computer screen? The mathematics are too complicated to explain here, but you can look at the logic of how it all works and gain a basic understanding.

Remember that each of our eyes sees in a conical field of view. Figure 5.1 shows the difference in the size that an object appears as a function of its distance from us. W_1 is equal to W_2 and represents the width of the box. L_1 and L_2 are different lengths and represent the width of our field of view at distances D_1 and D_2, respectively. To our brain, which inherently knows nothing of 3-D, the lengths L_1 and L_2 are the same, because they are representative of the maximum field of view. In this case, W_2 would appear much shorter than W_1. In effect, the brain tries to make lines A_1 and A_2 parallel, resulting in an image represented by figure 5.2.

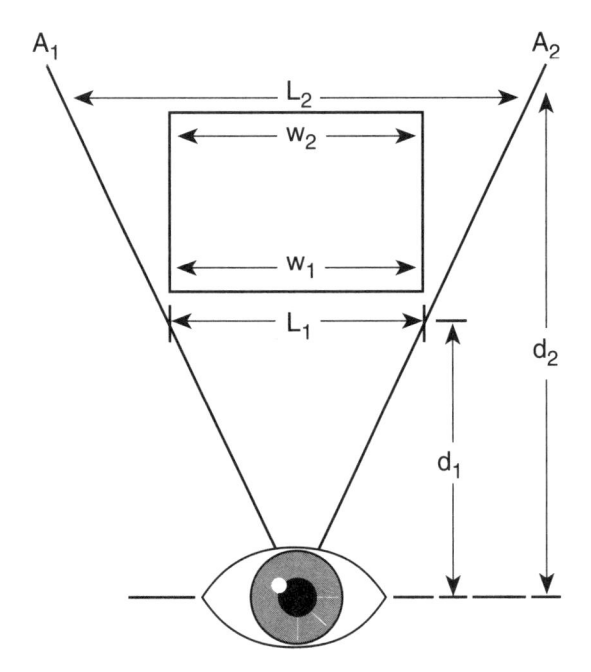

Figure 5.1

Perspective vision.

3-D PROGRAMS AND ILLUSION TECHNIQUES

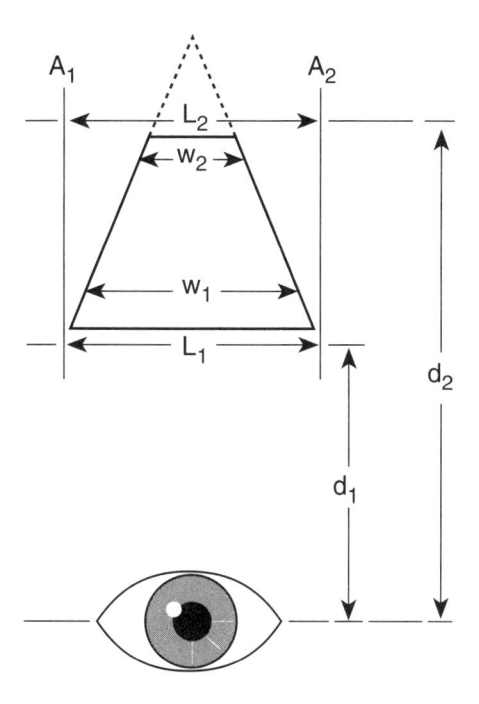

Figure 5.2

A parallel field of view.

If you look straight ahead, you get no feeling of seeing in a cone. You merely see straight ahead. The difference is that figure 5.1 represents a three-dimensional view and figure 5.2 represents a two-dimensional representation of that view. By making the lines A_1 and A_2 parallel, we have flattened out our world. The other changes (W_2 being shorter than W_1, for example) must be made to compensate for it.

If we reverse this concept, we get 3-D to 2-D projection. Look at figure 5.3, in which X, Y, and Z represent coordinate axes. The viewing plane is called the *projection plane*. If we draw straight lines from each important point on the object to our eye, or center of projection, the point where they pass through the projection plane forms an image which we call a *one-point perspective* projection.

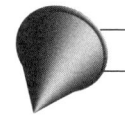

For point of discussion, compare figure 5.1 and figure 5.2 again. In figure 5.1, the lines that define the sides of the box are parallel, but A_1 and A_2 come to a point. In figure 5.2, the lines A_1 and A_2 are parallel, and if we extend the lines that define the sides of the box out behind the box, they converge at the vanishing point. This is called one-point perspective because only those lines which are parallel to the Z-axis converge at the vanishing point. If the lines parallel to the Z-axis converge at infinity, it is called a *parallel projection*.

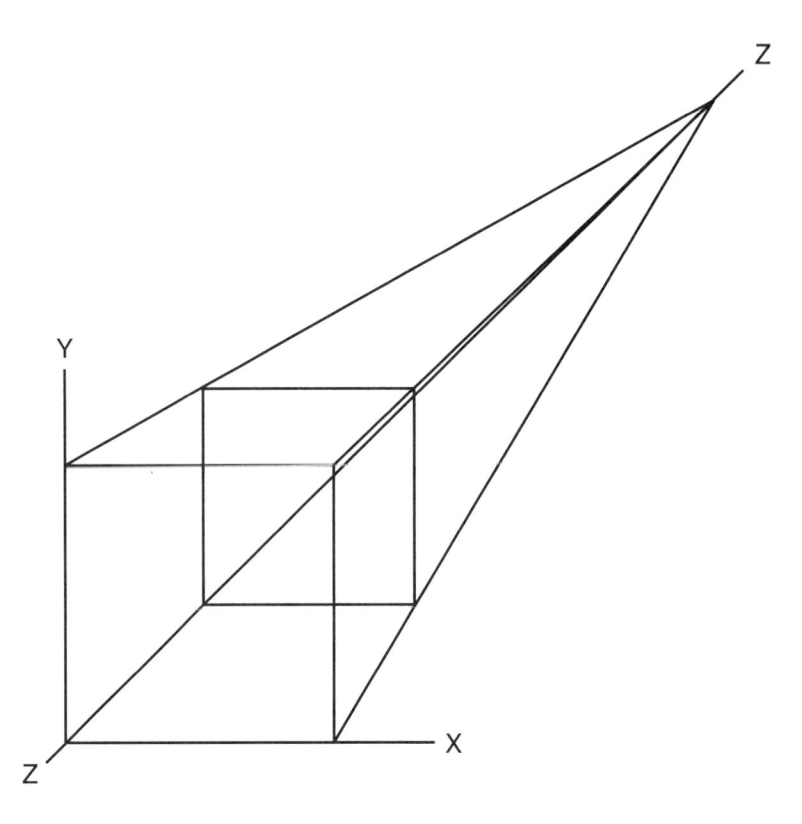

Figure 5.3

One-point perspective.

Perspective projections carry a label that tells how many axes converge. As you have seen, one-point perspective converges on one axis. Two-point perspective, then, must converge on two axes. Look at figure 5.4. The X-axis lines converge and the Z-axis lines converge. This type of illustration is more realistic than one-point perspective because usually, objects you view are not perfectly aligned with their projection plane. In the real world, all three axes converge.

Three-point perspective is very difficult to draw, however, and the technique is usually not used for illustration purposes. In advertising, engineering, and architecture, two-point perspective is the most common form of illustration.

3-D PROGRAMS AND ILLUSION TECHNIQUES

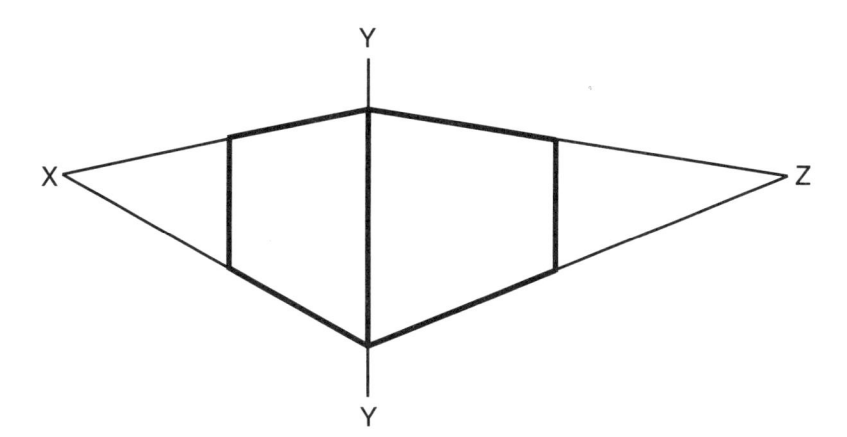

Figure 5.4

Two-point perspective.

When it comes to computer graphics—specifically 3-D programs, which generate perspective images automatically—three-point perspective is no problem. All the complications of drawing are done with mathematics inside the computer. By feeding sets of three-dimensional data into a formula, the computer can generate the two-dimensional projections very quickly and with near-perfect accuracy. This is the first step in three-dimensional modeling.

Three-dimensional modeling programs (some also have renderers attached, but more on this later) operate on data sets. These data sets are usually just lists of coordinates in X,Y, Z space, similar to the examples in figures 5.3 and 5.4. One at a time, the program goes down the list and generates a projection to our viewing plane (computer screen), then draws the object by turning on little points of light, or *pixels*. There are many other tricks used along the way to help make the image easier to view. One of these is *backplane removal* (see fig. 5.5). Backplane removal means that any part of the object that is hidden by the front should not be projected.

There are many techniques for backplane removal, but the simplest to understand is *Z-buffering*. In Z-buffering, a separate screen buffer is kept in computer memory which contains the depth value of each individual pixel on the screen. As the computer goes down the list of coordinates, projecting them onto the screen, it keeps track of the Z value that coincides with each X,Y point. If this X,Y is encountered again during the process and the Z value is closer to us than the previous value, it is replaced. This way, only the points which coincide with the Zs that are closest to us are actually drawn, thus hiding previous points (see fig. 5.6).

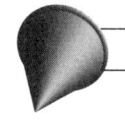

Figure 5.5

A cube before and after back-plane removal.

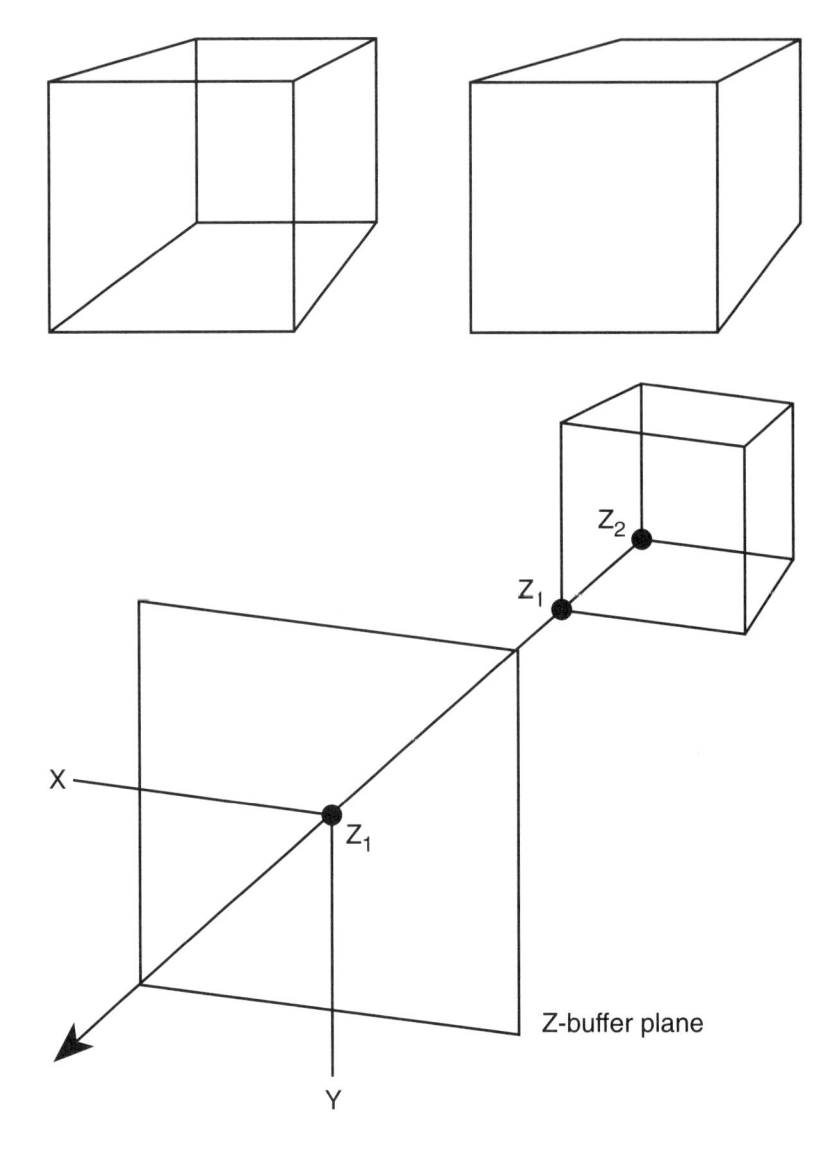

Figure 5.6

How a point on the screen is kept in a Z-buffer.

This technique is fast and easy to implement in a computer program, but it has two major side effects. The first is that it takes much extra memory. A separate memory buffer must be maintained that is the same size as the screen. The second is that because the relationships between adjacent pixels are not maintained, *aliasing* occurs. In very high-resolution images, this is not a problem; however, in normal computer resolutions, aliasing has the effect of

3-D PROGRAMS AND ILLUSION TECHNIQUES

making the images have hard, jagged edges. There are special anti-aliasing techniques employed by most 3-D programs, but they have a difficult time with Z-buffering.

Shading Models

After the computer modeling program has generated a projection, the image needs to be colored in order to look real. In this case, real means giving it the monocular cues that make it look like a three-dimensional object. The most obvious monocular cue is shading. Light is reflected from objects, and that reflected light is what allows us to "see" the object. Portions of the object in the direct light appear brighter than those in shadow or angled away from us. To simulate real-world lighting, a 3-D program must bounce light off the object. There are three basic ways of doing this on the computer. Each involves a different degree of difficulty to implement it; however, as the difficulty increases, so does the realism of the results.

Flat Shading

A 3-D object in computer memory is made up of *faces*. Faces are polygons that are defined by the edge points of an object, or *vertices*. In figure 5.7, the faces are spaces between the lines in the sphere. Notice that the number of faces is definitive of how detailed we want the drawing. Because computers are not infinitely fast, we must impose some limits on the definition of the image. In the case of our sphere, more faces will make the object look smoother. With the various shading models, however, you will see that this isn't necessary.

Flat shading means that the computer will calculate the normal vector of each face (the vector which points away from the face in a direct perpendicular to its surface plane), compare it to the angle of the light hitting it, and shade it with an intensity that is representative of the angle between *angle of incidence* and *surface normal*. This sounds complicated, but what it really means is that if a line drawn perpendicular to the face is parallel to and opposite in direction to the light ray, it will be illuminated at full intensity. As this angle

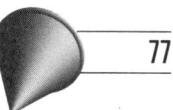

II USING THE COMPUTER FOR 3-D VISUALIZATION

grows, the intensity is reduced. If the surface normal and light ray are parallel and in the same direction, it means the surface is facing directly away from the light and therefore, no light falls on it. The results of flat shading are shown in figure 5.8.

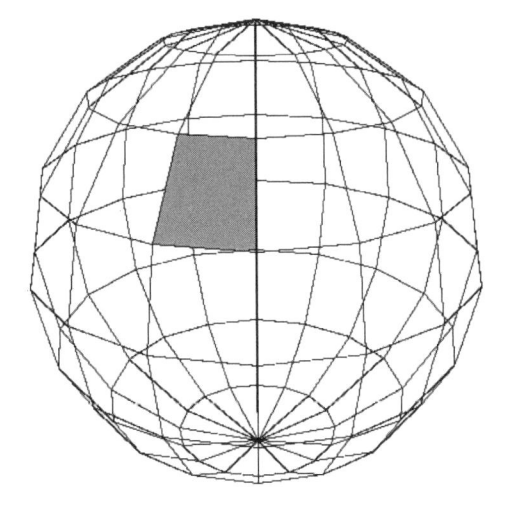

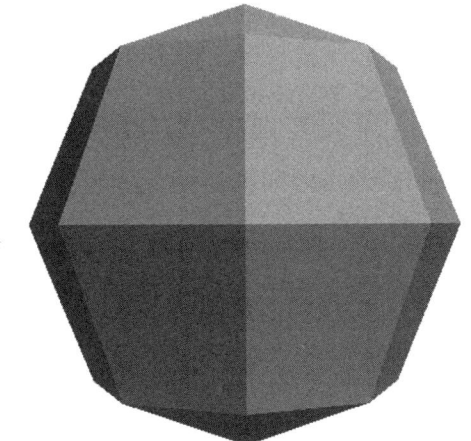

Figure 5.7

A wire-frame sphere with one face shaded.

Figure 5.8

A flat-shaded sphere.

The biggest drawback of flat shading is that the edges between faces are harsh because there is no smooth gradation between intensities. In the sphere example, this could be alleviated by making the faces smaller and smaller until they were only single pixels on the screen.

But if we did this, the number of points (and thus, the calculation time) would be so big that the computer would take too long to render the image.

Gouraud Shading

Gouraud shading, named after its inventor, H. Gouraud, solves some of the problems of flat shading. Instead of taking each face, calculating its surface normal and then coloring the face all one color, Gouraud shading varies the shading across the surface according to the following four-step method:

1. First, as in flat shading, surface normals are calculated.

2. Vertex normals are calculated by averaging the surface normals of each polygon which contributes to a particular vertex.

3. The intensity of those vertices is calculated in the same way that the flat-shaded polygons are calculated, by comparing it to the angle of light incidence.

4. Finally, the polygons are linearly smooth-shaded using the vertex intensities as limits.

This method is diagrammed in figure 5.9, and the results are shown in figure 5.10.

In figure 5.9, N_1-N_4 are the surface normals of each of the four faces that are adjacent to the vertex. N_0 is the average of N_1-N_4.

The drawback to Gouraud shading in the sphere example is that although the shading on each polygon is better than flat shading, it still is not realistic because the shading model is a linear one. In other words, the change in intensity from one vertex to another is calculated in a linear manner. Because the sphere is a curved surface, this model is not completely accurate. This technique reduces some of the edge problems encountered in flat shading, but there is still not a completely smooth transition between faces.

II USING THE COMPUTER FOR 3-D VISUALIZATION

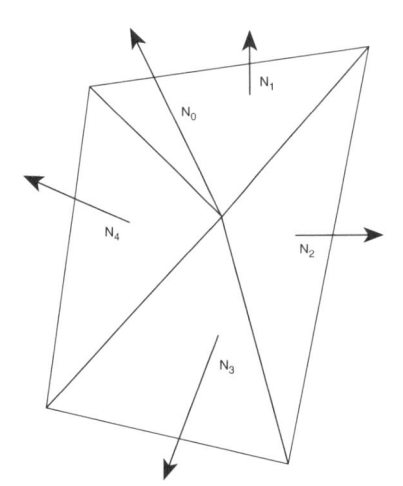

Figure 5.9

Vertex normal calculation.

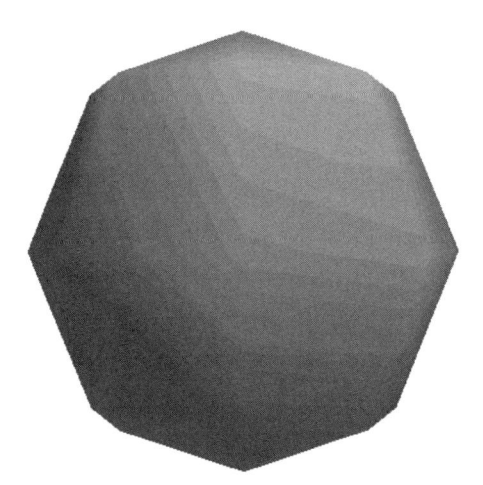

Figure 5.10

A Gouraud-shaded sphere.

Phong Shading

In 1975, Phong Bui-Tuong created a model for *normal-vector interpolation shading*. This is a mouthful, so the computer graphics community decided to call it Phong shading, after its inventor. Phong shading is similar to Gouraud shading except that rather than a linear interpolation between edges, the intensity at each interpolated normal is calculated and then shaded as the computer processes each scan-line. In flat shading and Gouraud shading, polygon surface normals are constant. In Phong shading, the normals are always being calculated through interpolation (see fig. 5.11, in which *N* stands for the vertex normal). This results in a smooth change in intensity (if the surface is in fact smooth).

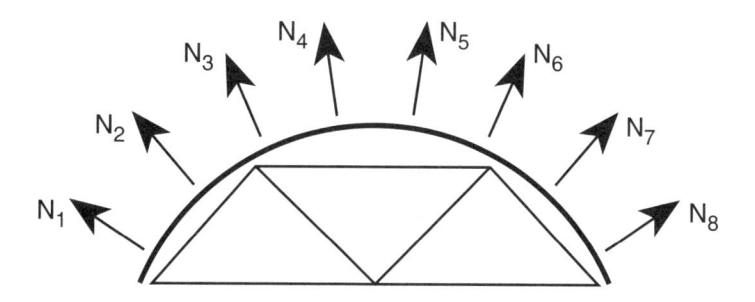

Figure 5.11

An interpolated normal calculation.

The light is reflected in such a way as to emulate real-world lighting effects. Because the interpolation is done in three dimensions, the intensity projections of the shading model parallel the perspective projections of the object.

It should be noted that interpolating a normal at each pixel that the computer draws is time-consuming. Phong shading is the most realistic; however, when you're generating previews, flat shading and Gouraud shading can be far less expensive in computer time. Figure 5.12 shows a phong-shaded sphere.

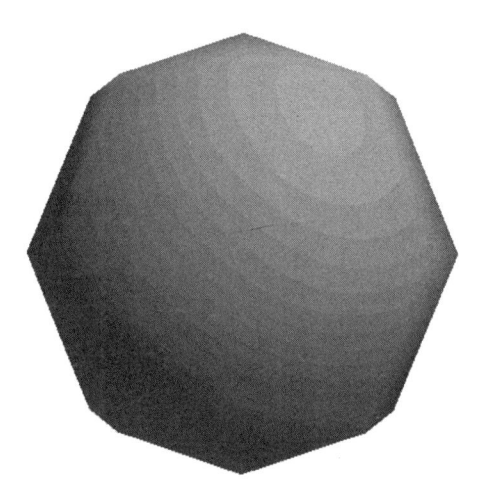

Figure 5.12

A Phong-shaded sphere.

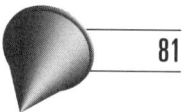

II USING THE COMPUTER FOR 3-D VISUALIZATION

Diffuse and Specular Reflection

The three shading models described in the preceding section deal with diffuse reflections of light. *Diffuse* reflections are defined as those in which objects reflect light equally in all directions. The effect of diffuse reflections is a matte object. A white light source bounced off a red apple reflects the red light in a diffuse manner, thus giving the apple its red color. But if the apple is shiny, we also see a white highlight spot. The shinier an object, the smaller its highlight spot is. This is because *specular highlights* are defined as those regions which reflect all source light according to normal laws of optics, or angle of incidence equals angle of reflection.

In other words, light coming from all directions reaches your eye, but a small portion is coming from a little piece of the apple that is directly in line with the source of light (see fig. 5.13). A mirror is a perfect specular reflector. All incident light is reflected perfectly. In the apple example, only at the point on the surface where the angles match up is specularity achieved.

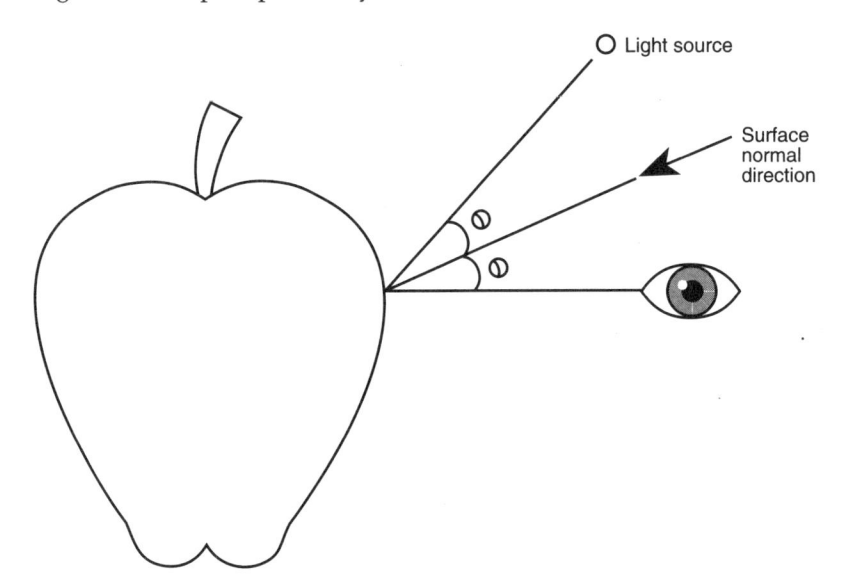

Figure 5.13

Specular reflection diagram.

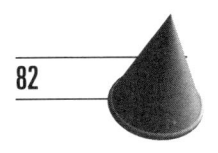

There are complicated mathematics involved for different materials, and these can be programmed into the computer. Visually, the way an apple reflects light is different than the sphere in our previous examples. We assumed no specular reflection when the spheres

3-D PROGRAMS AND ILLUSION TECHNIQUES

were rendered. In other words, they are not shiny like the apple. To keep this book simple, we will stick to the sphere example. Figure 5.14 shows the now-familiar sphere with the addition of a specular highlight. Notice how it now looks shiny.

Figure 5.14

A sphere with specular reflection.

Shadows

Shadows are calculated in much the same way as backface removal. Hidden-surface removal subroutines keep track of which faces are hidden from the viewer, and shadow programs keep track of which faces are hidden from the light source. Calculating shadows is a relatively easy task. Faces that are visible by both the viewer and the light source are not in shadow. Those that are visible to the viewer and not to the light source are darkened. This model for shadows works fine for point light sources.

What is not so simple is how to soften the edges of the shadows to simulate a realistic effect. The soft edges of shadows in the real world are due to light being reflected at odd angles from the edges of the objects which cast them, as well as the surface qualities of the reflected surface. A sharp-edged object casting a shadow on a shiny surface will have sharp edges, naturally. Another factor contributing to the complication is multiple light sources of varying types.

Shadows need only be calculated once for a particular scene, even if you move the point of view, or camera. This isn't obvious, but if you think of the shadows as being calculated as a result of the light source, they need to be recalculated only if the light source moves, not if the camera moves. Many sophisticated software programs use this technique when generating animation sequences to help reduce rendering times. They use a shadow buffer, similar in concept to the Z-buffer.

Other Properties

Many other properties contribute to the realism and thus the 3-D quality of images we generate on the computer. Transparent materials reflect only a portion of the light that hits them. *Transparent* materials are defined as those that transmit specular light. Glass and some polished plastics are examples of transparent materials. Their surfaces are very smooth, and if it weren't for reflections of surrounding objects, we might not even see them.

Translucent materials are those which transmit diffuse light. This diffuse property is due to surface irregularities. The effect is that light is scattered similarly in all directions, like the matte reflections in the apple example.

Another property of transparent and translucent materials is *refraction*. Refraction is a property of materials that bends light as it passes through it. Because refraction is an additional property (glass also transmits and reflects light), a transparent or translucent object becomes a new source of light rays and thus can be termed self-illuminating. Figure 5.15 shows how light is passed through a piece of glass with and without refraction.

Ray Tracing

The only way to properly calculate refraction is through a process called *ray tracing*. Ray tracing can be thought of as a highly specialized form of Phong shading in which every point is treated as a

3-D PROGRAMS AND ILLUSION TECHNIQUES

specular reflection. Each light ray is traced as it bounces from object to object in the scene. The difference is that Phong shading occurs in a scan-line processor, and ray tracing must do calculations which might cause the rays of light to jump all over the scene and cannot be processed in a linear fashion.

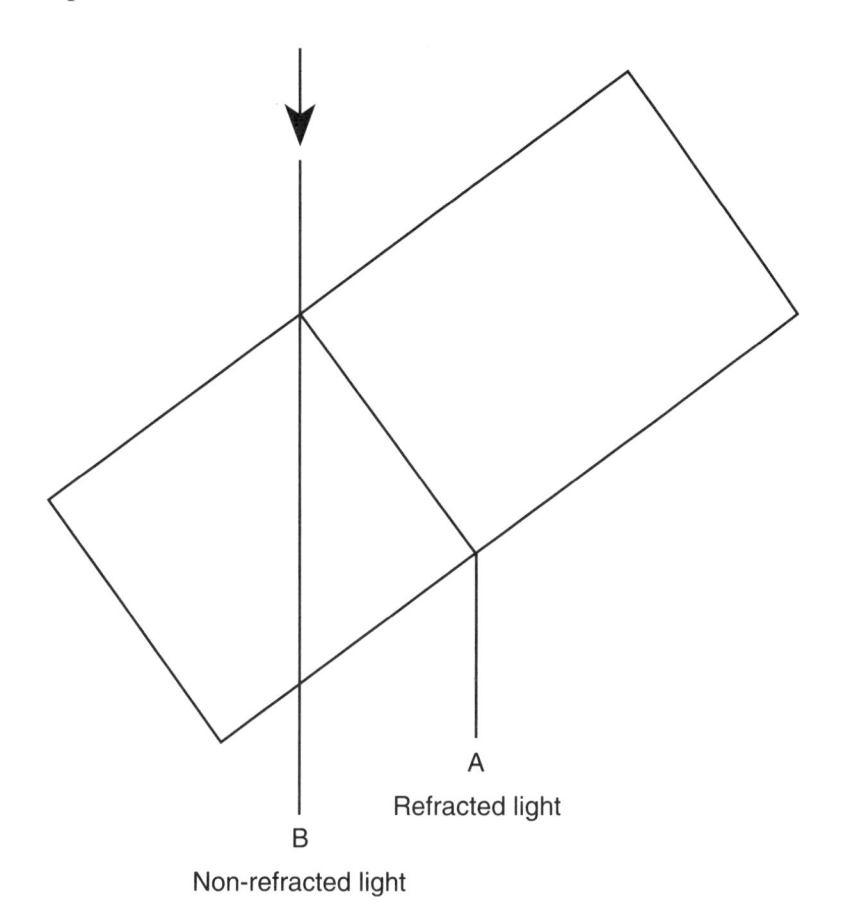

A
Refracted light

B
Non-refracted light

Figure 5.15
Refraction.

Ray tracing employs some very complicated mathematics, but a very simple idea. The basic idea is to trace each ray of light backward from the eye (the camera viewpoint in a 3-D program) to its source. The complication comes when you realize that each ray of light you see is made up of three components of light: spectrally reflected rays, refracted rays, and diffuse reflected rays. Tracing backward leads to a complex tree structure of source rays. To help minimize the complication, diffuse rays are omitted from the

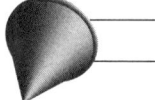

II USING THE COMPUTER FOR 3-D VISUALIZATION

analysis. This is because in reality, each ray of incident light that falls on an object is diffusely reflected an infinite number of times. This would be impossible to trace, so objects are usually colored with the diffuse color, then ray-traced for reflections and refraction.

Look at figure 5.16. Note the location of the eye. We will trace backward from this location to all the sources. Notice that there are three surfaces in this scene and three primary light sources. The surfaces are labeled Surface 1, Surface 2, and Surface 3. The light sources are labeled similarly. Note that surface 2 is opaque and that surfaces 1 and 3 are transparent.

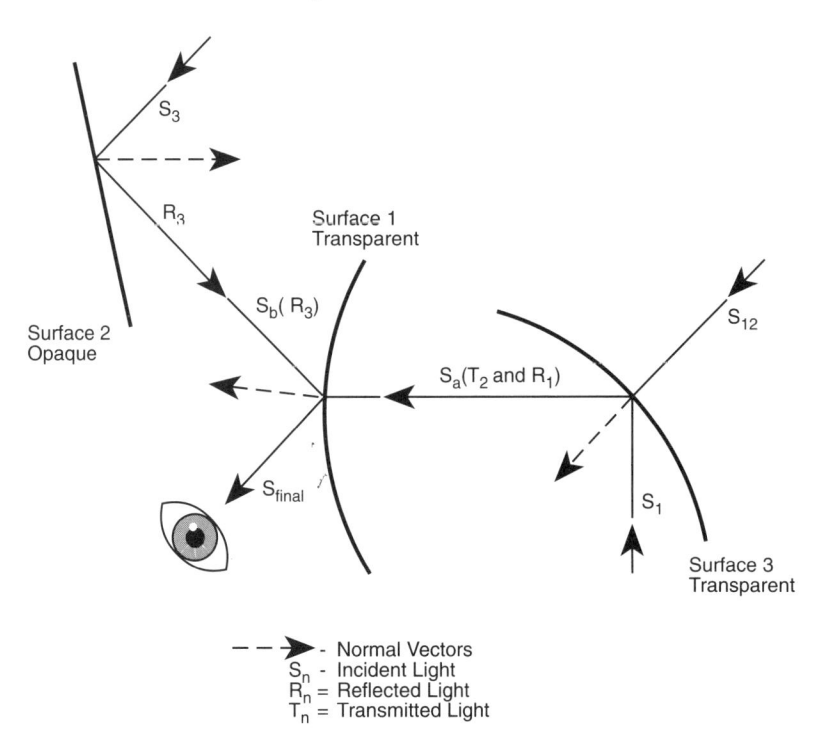

Figure 5.16

Ray tracing tree diagram.

Tracing backward from the eye, you see that S_{final} is composed of reflected light (S_b) and refracted light (S_a). Looking to the left side of the diagram, you see that S_b is actually R_3, which is the reflected light from source 3, reflected off surface 2. Similarly, S_a is a combination of the transmitted (refracted) light from S_2 and the reflected light from S_1. This theory is applied backward until either a light source is reached or the maximum number of reflections set in the program is reached.

3-D PROGRAMS AND ILLUSION TECHNIQUES

Other complications in ray tracing include keeping track of only those rays which pass through the center of projection and the projection plane. They are the only ones that need to be calculated because they are the only ones that are visible. In an array of pixels that is X by Y in size, the minimum number of rays that must be calculated is (X+1)(Y+1). Each of these rays must be tested for intersection with objects in the scene, then the reflection paths must be traced. Ray tracing also handles shadows differently than scan-line algorithms. If a ray is being traced around a scene, places where it is obscured are potential areas for shadow.

It is easy to see why ray tracing is slow. It does, however, provide the most realistic rendering model.

Other Surface Details

Other surface abnormalities may enter into your program's ability to properly reproduce the real world. These include bumpy surfaces, irregular surfaces, substances such as oil, and textures that are not clearly mathematically definable. Often, *fractal* techniques (see Chapter 8) are used to simulate real-world conditions which are not otherwise mathematically definable. Fractals have been successfully used to model liquids, mountains, and other apparently random surfaces. When the surface you are modeling is only slightly irregular, you can use special techniques to create very realistic simulations.

Texture mapping is a technique that is applied in all scan-line renderers to produce realistic surfaces. Texture mapping means that a texture in the form of a bitmap is applied to the polygons and faces of an object, like applying a cover to a baseball. There are two steps involved in creating a texture-mapped object. The first is to fix the edges of the map so that it doesn't move. If you want a wooden ball to roll across the floor, the wood grain would move with the ball as it rolls. This is done by applying *mapping coordinates* to the object which act like little anchor points to keep the map in place as it is rendered with a camera at any angle. If the edges were not anchored, the map would slide around the object and would not look realistic.

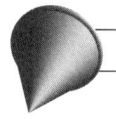

The second step is to apply the map itself. A bitmap (which is usually scanned in or hand-drawn) represents a pixel-by-pixel reference to the original object. This means that when the renderer is processing a particular pixel, it calculates the intensity from the lights and other contributing factors and applies it to a reference pixel in the texture map, then plots the pixel in the scene. The effect is similar to wrapping a planar object (a sheet of aluminum foil) around a 3-D object (a potato). The difference is that in the mathematical world of computers, the edges line up perfectly! There are companies that specialize in generating texture map materials which line up at all four edges so that seamless textures are created.

Another aspect of texture mapping that is important is *tiling*. Tiling refers to the number of times a particular map is repeated, edge to edge, during the rendering process. If you have a texture map that is a 2×2 black and white check, but want to render a real chess board, you need to tile it 4×4 to get the right number of squares. This is usually a simple parameter in 3-D programs.

Bump mapping is a variation on texture mapping used to generate depth effects in certain situations in which modeling the real object would be too complicated or too time-consuming. Bump mapping is a trick we play on our eyes to make them think that the surface we are looking at is bumpy, when in actuality it is flat. This is done by performing texture mapping operations with an additional reference map called a bump map. If you are shading an object with Phong shading, as each pixel's intensity is calculated, it can be modified by an intensity multiplier found in the bump map. For example, if you wanted the sphere to look bumpy, you could make a bump map of dark circles on a white background. Each screen pixel intensity the renderer calculates is modified using the value of the corresponding pixel in the bump map. The result is highlighted and darkened areas which make the object look bumpy (see fig. 5.17).

Objects rendered with bump mapping are useful only if viewed from the correct angle. For example, if you model the routed edges on kitchen cupboards with bump mapping, they appear realistic when viewed from the front. However, if you view them from the side, you don't see the edges. The cupboard door appears to be rectangular. Bump mapping does not affect the geometry of the scene, only the visual appearance. Some movement is possible, but a primarily straight-on view yields the best overall results.

3-D PROGRAMS AND ILLUSION TECHNIQUES

Figure 5.17

A bump-mapped sphere.

Reflectance mapping is a technique used by scan-line renderers to simulate the effect that ray tracers get from non-flat reflecting objects. By pre-rendering a frame from the point of view of the object, then texture mapping that frame onto the object, the object looks as though it is reflecting the scene. This technique is much faster than ray tracing. It is also used for generating other material simulations. There are several different types of reflectance mapping. Spherical reflectance mapping takes the reference bitmap and distorts it into a large sphere which surrounds the object it is to be mapped onto. It then maps it to the surface in a similar fashion to texture mapping, except that mapping coordinates are not used because reflections would move relative to the object if the object moved. The anchor points of texture mapping would prohibit this.

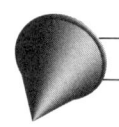

Another type of reflectance mapping is *cubic environment mapping*. This provides a much more realistic-looking rendering than spherical reflection. In cubic environment mapping, each of the six sides of a virtual cube that surrounds the object is mapped onto its faces. This type of reflectance mapping is superior for scenes that require real reflective surfaces such as mirrors, because the reflections are void of the aberrations that result from spherical approximations. A variety of this model is automatic cubic environment mapping, in which instead of the user specifying the six maps that represent the cubic environment, they are calculated from the actual environment. This works only on objects that are surrounded on all sides by other parts of the computerized 3-D world.

Opacity mapping enables you to generate a partially transparent object. Similar to bump mapping, the intensity of the reference map is used to determine the degree of transparency of the object being mapped. An intensity of zero means the object is completely transparent, and full white (full intensity) means that the object should be opaque at that location. As in bump mapping, the renderer goes about its job rendering pixel by pixel. As it does, it uses the reference pixels from the opacity map to set the transparency level. This is a very useful technique for generating effects that would be much more complicated to produce in geometry, such as irregular holes in irregular objects and soft, transparent edges. A 2×2 checkerboard opacity map applied to the sphere looks like figure 5.18.

Figure 5.18

An opacity-mapped sphere.

One of the most exciting aspects of texture mapping and its variations is using a combination of all the techniques simultaneously. By choosing a texture, such as marble, then bump mapping it to make it look rough, then reflectance mapping it to make it look shiny and reflective, then using opacity maps to make it look like pieces are missing, you can create a very interesting object. The combinations are limitless. Even though critics claim that ray tracing is the only way to generate completely realistic renderings, texture mapping variations can be pretty impressive in their own right.

3D Studio from Autodesk takes it all one step further. Most 3-D software packages allow you to generate and combine these texture mapping effects; however, 3D Studio enables you to animate them. By combining a sophisticated animation tool such as Autodesk Animator Pro with 3D Studio, a moving bump map or opacity map can be generated. All this means is that a sequence of frames is applied one at a time to the frames that result from the rendering. In other words, a different frame is used as a texture, bump, opacity, or reflectance map for each frame of a rendered animation sequence. Although this is theoretically possible with other animation packages, it is an automatic feature of 3D Studio.

Environmental Effects

All of the elements of computer-generated 3-D images mentioned thus far have dealt with generating the world, then bouncing light off of it and looking at the results. We have gone through the process of generating an object, shading it, and rendering it. What we haven't included are effects on the light before it reaches the object.

The atmosphere of the real world is constantly changing. Sunsets on the California coast are quite different than in the frozen Arctic. The way that natural lighting bounces around in a smoky bar room is different than spotlights in a model home. To properly model the real world, and thus fool our eyes into thinking we are seeing 3-D, requires the application of atmospheric effects.

Heat is a big factor in the way objects appear on the horizon. We have all looked out on a hot summer day and seen the heat waves rising. How did it effect what you saw? The horizon typically fades in haze. This is because the more atmosphere we look through, the more impurities we see. Weather also has an effect. Looking through a driving rain, heavy fog, or blinding snow storm all affect what we see and evaluate. Fortunately, computers simulate these phenomena easily. With the proper adjustments, almost any real-world environmental condition can be simulated.

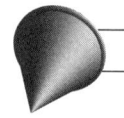

Summary

Even without cyclopean vision, seeing in 3-D is possible through the use of monocular cues. The computer is becoming an increasingly popular tool for generating 3-D environments. Visual monocular cues such as shadows and highlights are easily created through a variety of mathematical computer processes. A multitude of 3-D programs are available on all platforms with which you can mold, model, manipulate, and render your world as you see it.

Although a big drive in 3-D modeling and rendering software is real-world simulation, another push is going toward surrealistic work. The computer enables us to put cameras where we never thought they'd go. It is interesting to make a computer create realistic 3-D environments for educational and informative purposes, but it is usually not cost-effective to generate computer images when a live video shot is possible.

Model SF2HGS
ImageReader GS™

INCLUDES WINDOWS COMPATIBLE IMAGE EDITING AND OCR APPLICATIONS

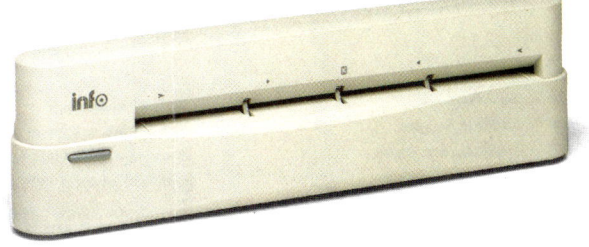

INTRODUCING POWER SCANNING!

With Info's ImageReader GS™ linked to your personal computer and printer, you'll have a state-of-the-art scanning system at your fingertips. Scan and manipulate your images and photos, then incorporate them into your document imaging, word processing, desktop publishing, multimedia productions, and fax communications.

How? It may be compact, but the ImageReader is a powerhouse! It's a full page, 400 dpi scanner with true 256 gray scale capability, 8-bit interface card, and a TWAIN-compliant driver.

And Info has bundled ImageReader GS with cutting-edge software to turn your computer into a paperless office:

Info Technician is the first diagnostic installation program ever included with a scanner to help you easily configure and install the ImageReader GS.

Recognita Plus OCR (Optical Character Recognition). This user-friendly OCR program captures text and data for import into nearly 30 word processing applications. Recognita Plus recognizes widely used fonts and can learn almost any font style.

iPhoto Plus image editing software provides specialized tools for joining parts of an image, combining images or selected parts of images, and adjusting the brightness, contrast, gamma, saturation, and hue of scanned images.

Interested in more details? See the other side.

For more information call 1-800-775-7576

IMAGERY 6

...ype of
...e left eye
...es make
...nore
...es into a
...d to
...n such a
...ation.

...are
...eye
...ed, the
combination of the two is called an *anaglyph*. The result looks like an out-of-focus image with a red ghost on the right and a blue ghost on the left. The amount of this "ghosting" depends on the distance the objects are from us. Objects at the focal length or registration point are not separated at all. Objects beyond that are separated with blue on the left and red on the right. The greater the color separation, the further away the object is. For near objects (those closer to us than the focal plane), the greater the separation, the closer the object is to us.

When this special anaglyph image is viewed with a pair of glasses that have the left eye filtered with a red transparent material and the right eye filtered with blue, only the components of the image intended for each eye reach it. In other words, the right eye views only the right image and the left eye views only the left image. This is an easy task with black-and-white images because the result is a composite of red and blue and the picture integrity remains intact. Color images provide special problems, as you will see later. The special red and blue glasses used to view the image are called *anaglyph glasses*. The separation your brain sees as it tries to put the image back together is similar to looking at the real world and getting two different inputs.

Anaglyphs on a Computer Screen

When you view anaglyphs printed on paper, the image is flat and dull. By contrast, the computer provides a wonderful viewing mechanism for anaglyphs. The radiance of illuminated phosphor enhances the otherwise drab images. Typically, anaglyph images are missing a great deal of the brilliance of their full-color stereo pair counterparts; on a computer screen, however, they come to life. Radiating light provides a greater base for controllable brightness and contrast enhancement. Greater contrast also means enhanced monocular cues such as shadows and shading.

Another great advantage in viewing anaglyphs on a computer rather than printed on paper is the ability to adjust the color levels until you get a perfect match with the particular set of viewing glasses. A careful match means cleaner separation of the red and blue lines and thus, more accurate binocular re-creation. This process is demonstrated later in this chapter.

The mechanism for creating anaglyphs on computer from a black-and-white or color stereo pair is *digital image processing*. Images can be computer-generated or scanned in using a color scanner. Proper alignment must be maintained during the scanning process to ensure quality anaglyph reproduction.

When an image is scanned, the scanning software creates a *24-bit* or *true-color* image. This means that every pixel can have a different "true" color (each pixel is independent of every other pixel), and that pixel can be any of 16.7 million colors. Special portions of the program called *color reduction algorithms* reduce the colors in the image to a more manageable number, usually 256. These 256 colors are then converted into 256 different gray levels. Now all that is left to do is to tint each image to the proper shade of blue or red, then combine them into a composite image. This might sound like a complicated process to the digital image processing novice; however, most of these steps are automatic functions in most image processing software packages.

Color anaglyphs are also possible, thanks in part again to digital image processing. Because the colors on a computer screen are comprised of red, blue, and green components, these components are easily controlled to tint an image. If the green and blue are removed from the "red" image, and the red and part of the green are removed from the "blue" image, a composite that retains most of its original color is left. This process was documented by Dr. Stephen Erskine in England in 1991, who applied for a patent in the U.K. and for a U.S. extension. This process is virtually impossible in the darkroom unless filtering techniques are used, which have a tendency to degrade the original image.

Another advantage to using computers for image generation is in the automation of the entire process. Most sophisticated software packages (including almost all image processing packages) allow the generation of *macro* commands. Macros are simply a sequence of steps that you can teach the computer to remember, then to repeat on its own time. Through record and play macros, batch processing, or using run-time scripts, you can completely automate the process of generating anaglyphs on a computer.

Viewing Some Anaglyphs

The disk included with this book contains two high-quality anaglyph images. To install them on your computer, follow the installation instructions at the back of this book. After you have installed the software, get out your red and blue glasses and have some fun!

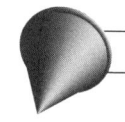

II USING THE COMPUTER FOR 3-D VISUALIZATION

To view the images, use the provided freeware picture view, PICEM.EXE. To use PICEM, type

```
CD \QUE3D\3DPICS
PICEM
```

You see a list of pictures. The anaglyphs start with the letters *ana*. Select the one you want to view using the arrow keys, then press Enter. To get the full 3-D effect, put on the anaglyph glasses included in this book and sit squarely in front of the image. Then move your head side to side and notice how the different portions of the image appear to move relative to one another, just as they would in the real world. Of course, this motion is limited, whereas in the real world you could literally walk around the entire scene. The effect is strong enough, however, to give you a 3-D feeling.

The first image is a photograph taken at St. Mawes Castle, England. The photograph is actually two photographs which make up a stereo pair. The pair was then scanned and converted to an anaglyph, again using digital image processing software. The color was removed before tinting, and then the brightness and contrast were adjusted to enhance the image. This image was taken using the *Erskine shift* technique. The technique was named after Dr. Stephen Erskine, although he probably didn't invent it. To take a decent stereo pair with only one camera, all you need to do is put your weight mostly on your left foot, take a picture, then shift your weight to your right foot and take another. The St. Mawes Castle image is proof that the technique works quite nicely!

The second image was generated by 3D Studio, a 3-D modeling, rendering, and animation software program from Autodesk. To generate the simulated 3-D effects, two separate cameras were set up to emulate the views from each eye. A separate image was generated for each eye, then the images were tinted and combined with image processing software as described earlier in this chapter. Notice how the effects of shadows, shading, and other lighting all contribute to the 3-D effect.

Go back and forth between the images and make mental notes of all the things in the image that contribute to its 3-D effect. In the computer-generated image, everything you see was created by the computer according to a complex set of mathematics. The photograph is the real world. How good a job did the computer do?

Enough experimentation, let's make an anaglyph of our own!

Making an Anaglyph

Viewing anaglyphs isn't always enough. You feel the real 3-D experience when you can control the parameters yourself. The best way to do this is to make an anaglyph of your own.

Techniques for 3-D Programs

3-D modeling and rendering programs such as those referred to in Chapter 5 simulate the world of 3-D by generating shading, shadows, and highlights, as well as environmental effects and other visual cues. To generate an image, the user must build a universe in 3-D coordinate space by creating objects, assigning materials to the objects, putting lights in the scene so that it is properly illuminated, then setting up a camera position so that the scene is created as though the user were at that camera location looking at the point in the scene where the camera is pointed. When the option to render the scene is selected, the computer does all of the work.

This process closely parallels the process a photographer goes through in the studio to create a custom shot for a client. The photographer must first build the props; decorate and paint them; turn on lights and adjust them for proper lighting, shadows, and shading; then set up the camera and take a shot. Many computer programs parallel real life in an attempt to make them easier to operate. In the case of 3-D programs, this technique works very well.

If you want to generate an anaglyph image, you must follow the same procedure that a photographer would in the studio. You set up two cameras and take two pictures that are a stereo pair. Then you process the pair into an anaglyph using one of the image processing techniques mentioned earlier. A discussion of how to properly set cameras follows in Chapter 7.

Designing for Anaglyphs

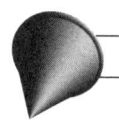

Anaglyphs are usually black and white stereo pairs tinted for the anaglyph gimmick. Designing in a 3-D program for anaglyph output should be considered the same as designing for black-and-white images. This means heavier contrast and sharper shadows than in color photography. The sharper the contrast between objects, the better the red and blue lines will separate and the better the 3-D effect is.

Although it is possible to generate color anaglyphs with many 3-D programs, not just any color stereo pair works well. Remember that to preserve color, some green is left in during the digital image processing. Objects that are sharply red or blue don't work, because the complimentary image is not visible when the red and blue separation is performed. It is best to generate images with colors that have a rich mix of red, green, and blue components, with none saturated too far in the red or blue direction.

Colors combine on a computer in an *additive* fashion, whereas in print they are *subtractive*. This means that if you add red, blue, and green together on computer, you get white. A mix of all colors on printed paper yields black. So the best mix of colors to generate an anaglyph that can be reconstructed without much loss of color would be with near equal parts of red, green, and blue. The more red, green, and blue, the brighter the image. The problem is that this equal mix of colors yields gray tones, so the benefit of having a color anaglyph is lost.

Making Your Own Anaglyphs with Anadraw

So just how do you go about generating an anaglyph? There are several methods. The easiest is by drawing one directly. When drawing anaglyphs, it is important to understand in advance what you are drawing and which portions of your image lie in front of the others. Usually, this is done by drawing in *planes*. This means that you predefine planes of depth and draw the objects in that plane with the same degree of separation.

Included on the disk at the back of this book is a program called Anadraw. Assuming you have installed the software properly (installation instructions are at the back of the book), change into the directory where the software is installed. If you used the default settings on the install program, this is drive C, subdirectory \3D.

ANAGLYPH IMAGERY

Type the following:

```
C:
CD \QUE3D
```

Now change into the subdirectory that contains the Anadraw software by typing

```
CD ANADRAW
```

Now, run the program by typing

```
ANADRAW
```

You should see a screen that looks like figure 6.1.

Figure 6.1

The Anadraw start-up screen.

The left side of the screen is the icon bar, and the right portion is the drawing area. The icons function as follows:

    CLR—Clears the screen

    ADJ—Adjusts the red and blue levels to match your anaglyph glasses

    DEMO—Runs a collection of sample images for testing

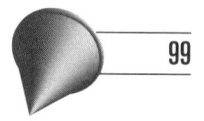

II USING THE COMPUTER FOR 3-D VISUALIZATION

4 through −4—Select the depth of your drawing or the separation of the red and blue lines

EXIT—Quits the program

The first thing you have to do when setting up to view anaglyphs is to adjust your screen colors to properly match your particular set of red and blue glasses. This is a relatively simple task on a computer palette-mapped system because all the software has to do is adjust the red or blue guns under user control until a proper match is found.

To set the color with Anadraw, scribble some lines on the screen with the default red/blue separation. Put on your red/blue glasses and then click the ADJ button. You see a dialog box with two sliders in it (see fig. 6.2).

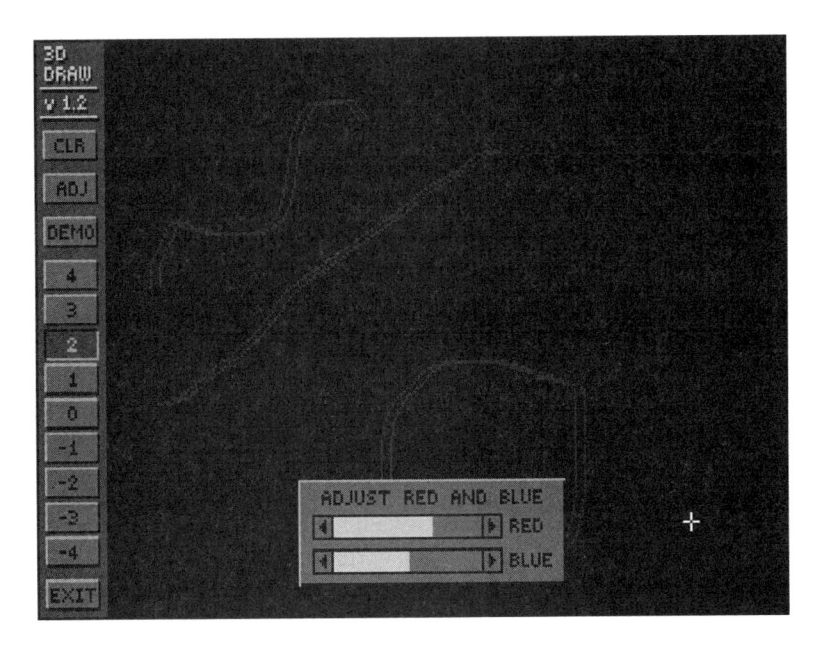

Figure 6.2

The red/blue adjustment box in Anadraw.

Click the arrows to the right and left of the red or blue sliders to adjust the saturation levels. When you have a perfect match, the lines you drew will have perfect convergence. This means that they should look like they were drawn with one line, because the red lens filters all the red light and the blue lens filters all the blue light. If you can still see a pair of lines, keep adjusting until they converge. For rapid adjustments, click in the slider area (where the white bar is). The slider jumps to the location you clicked. Note that you do not see any 3-D effect, because the lines you drew were all with the same separation. Without variation, there is no point of reference, and therefore no 3-D effect. When you have adjusted your colors, press any key to continue.

When working with anaglyphs on the computer screen, it is easiest to see the 3-D effects if a point of reference is made on the screen, telling your eyes the plane of the screen. This is done with the solid color magenta, which is a mix of red and blue (this is the color you see after the red/blue glasses converge the separated lines). To draw with magenta, select the number 0 from the list. The higher number you choose, the further into the screen the object you draw appears. For example, if you select 4, the object appears to be the maximum distance into the screen affordable by this simple program. If you select – 4, the object you draw appears to be closer to you than the screen.

In real-world anaglyphs (converted from photographs), the plane of reference is always the focal length of the lens of the camera that took the picture. Before you draw your own objects, try the demo by clicking the DEMO button.

The screen should now look like figure 6.3.

Adjust your position so that your head is approximately three feet from the screen. Now move your head from side to side. The concentric circles should look like the largest one is at the plane of the screen, and each successively smaller circle goes further and further into the screen, or away from you. If you are having trouble resolving the 3-D effect, try moving closer to or farther away from the screen. Move your head from side to side. When you have resolved the 3-D effect, press any key.

The circles should appear to come out of the screen toward you. Again move your head from side to side to get the full effect. Remember that if you cannot resolve the 3-D effect, you might be one of the people who simply cannot resolve 3-D images, or you might be slightly color-blind. Now try to make your own 3-D images. Start by selecting the 0 plane for reference. Draw a rectangle in the center of the screen. The screen should look something like figure 6.4.

II USING THE COMPUTER FOR 3-D VISUALIZATION

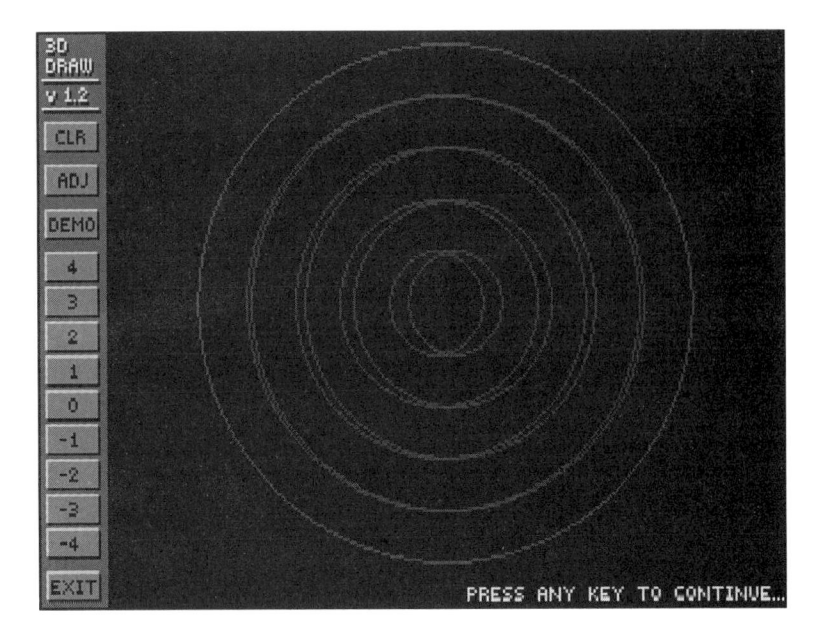

Figure 6.3

The first screen of DEMO.

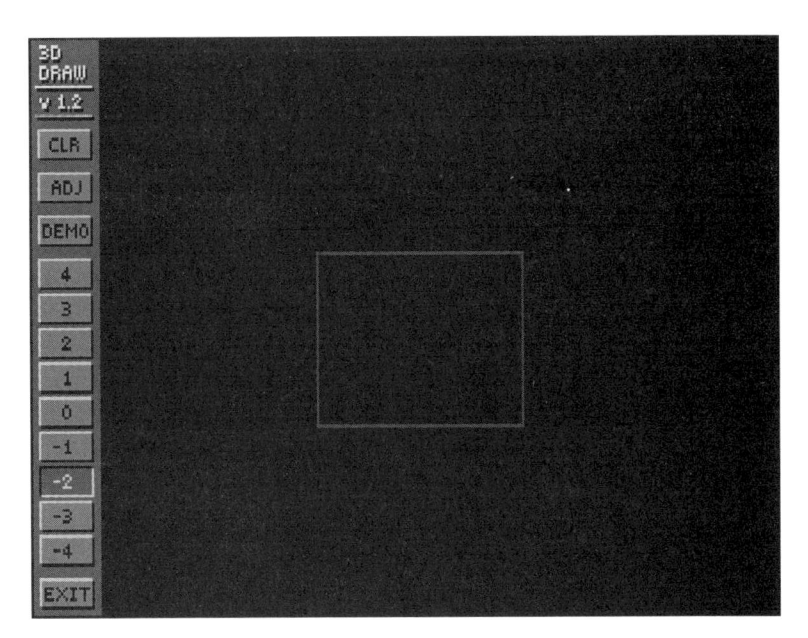

Figure 6.4

Setting the reference point.

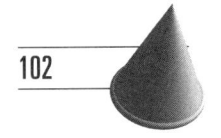

Click the 2 button and draw a smaller rectangle upward and to the left of your first rectangle. Then click the –2 button and draw a rectangle downward and to the right of the first one. Your screen should look like figure 6.5.

Figure 6.5
Your first anaglyph image.

Now put on your glasses and look at your masterpiece. The top left rectangle should look like it is further away than the screen, and the bottom right rectangle should look like it is closer to you. The center rectangle is, of course, at screen distance. Try other variations and see how dramatic an effect you can create. This time, do the drawing with the glasses on. It provides a new perspective on drawing! As you change screen depths, it appears as though you can draw under and over previously drawn lines.

Animating Anaglyphs

Another interesting way to view anaglyphs is when they are moving. It is sometimes easier to resolve three dimensions when the object is constantly changing. By varying the differences between the red and blue versions of an object according to predefined matrix mathematics, three-dimensional motion is simulated. A good example of this is the program called STEREO, by Schreiber Instruments, included on the software disk that comes with this book.

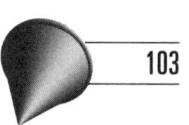

II USING THE COMPUTER FOR 3-D VISUALIZATION

Although the name STEREO might seem misleading because we are viewing anaglyph images, it is really a stereo drawing program. The program generates a stereo pair using two cameras, then renders the scene using techniques similar to those described in Chapter 5. The raw data for an object is mathematically projected into the 2-D plane of the computer. This is done twice, once for each camera location. Then each image in the stereo pair is encoded with red or blue and drawn on the screen. Because the program works with a limited set of data points, the math and the drawing can be done in real time and the screen updates are fast enough that you get smooth animation.

A technique called *page-flipping* is also used to help smooth the animation. Page-flipping means that the images aren't really drawn directly on the screen. They are drawn to a background buffer, then flipped out the front screen all at once. This way, you don't see the lines actually being drawn, and there is no flicker.

STEREO.EXE operates on any text file that fits the following description: The file should contain lines with x-y-z triplets, separated by spaces or tabs. A blank line indicates a start of a new *polyline*, and consecutive nonblank lines contain the vertices. The file must have the extension *.3D*.

For example, here is the data file for a cube:

CUBE.3D

−1	−1	−1
1	−1	−1
1	1	−1
−1	1	−1
−1	−1	−1
−1	−1	1
1	−1	1
1	1	1
−1	1	1
−1	−1	1

1	−1	−1
1	−1	1
1	1	−1
1	1	1
−1	1	−1
−1	1	1

This data doesn't tell you much. You can see the results faster by running it through STEREO.EXE. If you have not installed the software that came with this book, do so now by referring to the last page of this book. To run STEREO, change into the 3D directory by typing

```
C:
CD \QUE3D
```

Now change into the subdirectory that contains the STEREO software by typing

```
CD STEREO
```

Then run the program by typing

```
STEREO CUBE
```

Your screen should now have a rotating cube on it. While the cube is rotating, you can control its motion with the following keys:

Arrow keys—Change rotation direction

Shift-arrow keys—Pan the image around the screen

PgUp, PgDn—Zoom in or zoom out

+, −—Speed up and slow down

Home—Restores initial position

Shift-Home—Restores initial speed

End—Toggles auto-rotate on and off

Esc—Quits program and returns to DOS

While the cube is rotating, press Shift-PgUp to make it move toward you. Press Shift-PgDn to make it recede into the screen. Be sure to wear your red/blue glasses!

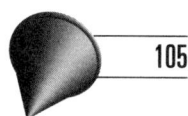

For more fun, try one of the other objects included in the demo. The more complex objects, such as contour, were created using another Schreiber product called SURF3D. SURF3D is used to create three-dimensional surfaces for various applications such as simulation and CAD. Some of the more interesting objects are as follows:

FISHNET.3D—A 3-D surface created with SURF3D

DODECA.3D—A dodecahedron that looks like a soccer ball

MOEBIUS.3D—The classic moebius strip

ROBOT.3D—A CAD drawing of a robot arm

OREGAMI.3D—Looks like a folded paper airplane

The file STEREO.DOC has instructions for using the program in conjunction with Autodesk AutoCAD Release 12. STEREO was originally designed for animating AutoCAD models. For more information about STEREO and other Schreiber CAD products, refer to Appendix A.

Summary

Stereo pairs can be combined to create anaglyph images by encoding the left and right images with red and blue tinting, then viewing them through red and blue glasses. This technique for single-image 3-D viewing has been around since about 1858, when D'Almeida first put red and green filters over a stereo projector. Anaglyphs have been used for large-format 3-D viewing for a long time because of the difficulties that arise when trying to resolve large-format dual images. X-rays, comic books, and many computer graphics games are available in anaglyph format.

The computer is a valuable tool for viewing anaglyphs for several reasons. The fact that the images are created with radiant light makes them easier to resolve. Because of the flexibility of computer graphics, the red and blue intensities of the image can be adjusted dynamically to accurately match the viewing glasses, thus giving the best possible 3-D resolution. The separate images of the stereo pair can be adjusted to provide optimum image separation without loss in image quality. Anaglyphs will provide an inexpensive, easy to implement 3-D viewing solution for some time to come.

Stereo Imagery on Computer

As you read in Chapter 3, stereo images have long been viewed using mechanical means. Recently, it has become popular to use the computer as a viewing device. This is partially because since so many 3-D images are generated by the computer, it seems logical to use the same computer to view them. There are many methods for converting and viewing images on a personal computer, and that is the focus of this chapter.

Graphics Hardware

In order to display an image in 3-D, you need proper graphics hardware. This includes a graphics processor card and display monitor. Graphics cards and monitors are in constant development as vendors try to improve on resolution, speed, and color.

II USING THE COMPUTER FOR 3-D VISUALIZATION

The Development of Adequate Computer Graphics Hardware

Since the development of the personal computer in the mid-1970s, graphics have been an obsession of both scientists and hobbyists. As soon as graphics were developed, the quest for realistic images began. The first circle soon developed into a sphere, rectangles became cubes, and the world around us was quickly modeled on a computer screen. (Chapter 5 details some of the techniques used for 3-D image generation.) Along the way, color digitizers were developed, which capture real life like digital cameras. Today, photographs are easily scanned into computer images.

Whereas software algorithms progressed at an astronomical pace, computer hardware evolved more slowly. The first Apple II computers were low-resolution and not very colorful. Early IBM PCs had only four colors and even lower resolution than the Apple. The Apple Macintosh had increased resolution, but was released initially in black and white. It wasn't until the mid-1980s that a reasonable standard was set that had both enough color and enough resolution to support photo-realistic images.

The minimum resolution and color depth for quality imaging is 640×480 pixels, with at least 256 colors from a substantially larger palette. With clever color reduction and dithering algorithms, photo realism was put in the mainstream of personal computing. Today, this is a minimum graphics configuration for any new personal computer sold. In fact, it is common to see true-color (16.7 million colors) and high-resolution (1280×1024 pixels) on low-cost computers sold through mass merchant channels. These resolutions and colors are manageable with today's very fast computers and large hard disk drives.

Resolution and Loss of Information

So why are resolution and color so important? Remember our discussions on what it takes to see in 3-D. You need accurate visual cues. If you are viewing stereo pairs, you need very accurate binocular separation for the brain to interpret the images correctly. Without enough pixels of resolution and differences in color, these cues may yield inaccurate results.

STEREO IMAGERY ON COMPUTER

Pixels on the computer screen are nothing more than digital approximations of the real analog world. The finer the approximation, the more accurate the reproduction (see fig. 7.1). This premise holds true on any digital technology. If the curve in figure 7.1 is divided into small enough pieces, it will, for all practical purposes, be exactly like the original curve.

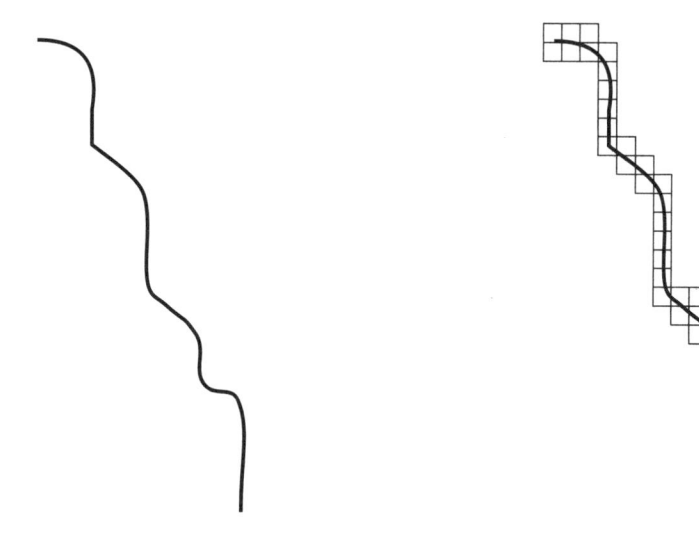

Figure 7.1
Converting analog into digital.

The trick is to get the resolution fine enough to be accurate, but no more. Finer resolution means more information to store and process; the data files get so large that managing them becomes prohibitive. It turns out that the combination of average monitor size (14 inches diagonal), the ability of the eye to resolve pixels at an average viewing distance, and the actual size of the pixels all combine so that a resolution of 640×480 pixels allows a reasonable compromise between visual accuracy and storage requirements. You can sometimes get the same effect with lower resolution if there is an increase in the number of colors.

When pixels are large (low resolution), the edges between them are more obvious if the colors differ in intensity. Look at figure 7.2. The top box has 21 pixels, 12 white and 9 black. It is obvious where the black and white pixels meet. This is an *aliased edge*.

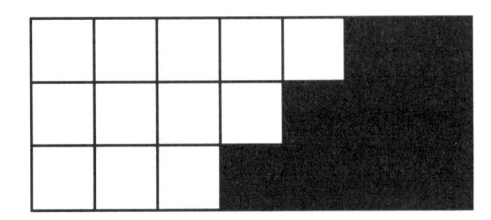

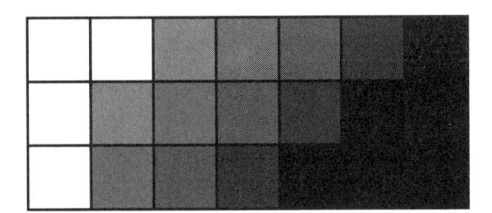

Figure 7.2

Aliasing and antialiasing.

The lower box has gray pixels between the white and black ones. This results in a smoother transition, which fools our eyes into thinking there is a smooth edge there, rather than a hard one. This technique is called *antialiasing*, and it is used to make low-resolution pictures look more realistic. This process happens automatically during the color scanning process, but it must be done algorithmically with a 3-D program that generates images. In either case, the result is an improved image, as far as our eyes are concerned.

Stereo Output from 3-D Programs

The best part about using computers for 3-D image generation is that it is possible to create unrealistic images. In other words, you can put a camera in places that would be very difficult in the real world. In Chapter 4, we briefly discussed *hypo-stereo*. To summarize, hypo-stereo is the result you get when viewing stereo pairs that were taken with cameras that are much closer together than your eyes. The resulting images are magnified proportionally with the actual separation. This condition is most often seen in stereo microscopy. When the camera separation is much larger than interpupilliary separation and the object of the image is at a great distance, a condition called *hyper-stereo* results. The result is that the images have a greater perceived depth than in reality.

A common method of generating hyper-stereo images is with aerial fly-bys. If successive images are taken from a moving helicopter or airplane that is parallel to the ground, the distance the plane travels between images is much greater than the distance between our eyes, so the ground pictures will look more 3-D than with the naked eye. If all images are flat at infinity, the ground must look quite flat from a high-flying airplane. But through the use of hyper-stereo, 3-D effects are generated.

It is easy to generate hyper-stereo images with a computer by simply moving the cameras far apart in the 3-D program. You can test this effect in Chapter 10 with the Vistapro fractal terrain generator. In most 3-D programs, such as 3-D Studio from Autodesk, multiple cameras may be set up and then rendered independently. By "cloning" a camera and moving it in a direction perpendicular to the first camera, left- and right-eye views may be set up automatically. The distance between cameras may be adjusted to compensate for normal stereo, hyper-stereo, or hypo-stereo. Although there are no specific parameters telling which camera separations yield the best results, the 3-D effect can be adjusted easily and then the images rerendered until the desired effect is achieved.

Stereo Separation

In Chapter 1, we discussed the basics of binocular vision. For an image to look "real," the parameters of "real" vision must be maintained. This means a camera separation of 65mm when the images are generated and an infinity separation of 65mm when the images are displayed. When taking stereo photographs, this is accomplished mechanically with a slide bar or specially modified stereo camera. When using a 3-D program on the computer, it becomes a more difficult task, because real-world coordinates are rarely used (except in architectural work). Usually, a coordinate system is set up with a random basis and objects are created relative to each other, rather than with reference to the real world. It really doesn't matter, however, if all you want is a generic 3-D effect. If you want realistic 3-D viewing, it is best to use a real coordinate system and thus, real camera separation.

After you have a stereo pair, you need to display it in such a way that it can be viewed on a computer screen. Unfortunately, this means either having two tall, skinny images or two images that are reduced in size (see fig. 7.3).

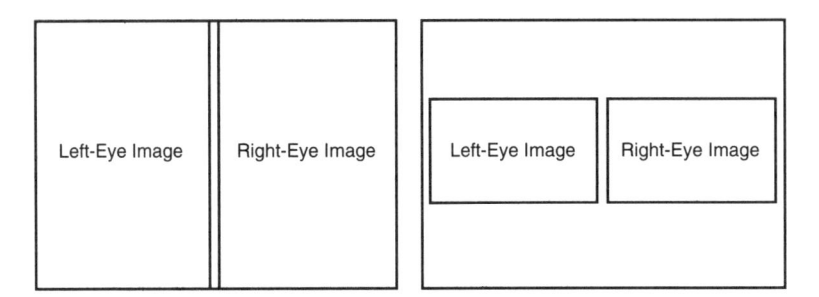

Figure 7.3

Stereo pair alignment.

There are no specific rules for setting up the images. As long as stereo effect can be realized, any orientation usually works. For normal stereo pairs, the following specifications in figure 7.4 should work. These specifications are for a 640×480 screen. Higher resolutions should be scaled up linearly. Displaying the images side-by-side and then using a reflecting stereoscope results in a very high-quality stereo pair.

Hands-on Examples

If you have an IBM PC or compatible with VGA graphics, you have adequate hardware to experiment with 3-D. This book comes with some sample stereo pairs, as well as a stereo drawing program. It's time to see for yourself what the fuss is all about.

Viewing Some Stereo Pairs

On the disk included with this book are several high-quality stereo pairs. To install them on your computer, follow the installation instructions at the back of the book. After you have installed the software, find a reflecting stereoscope, try the cross-eyed method described in Chapter 3, or try your hand at free-viewing, a description of which follows.

STEREO IMAGERY ON COMPUTER

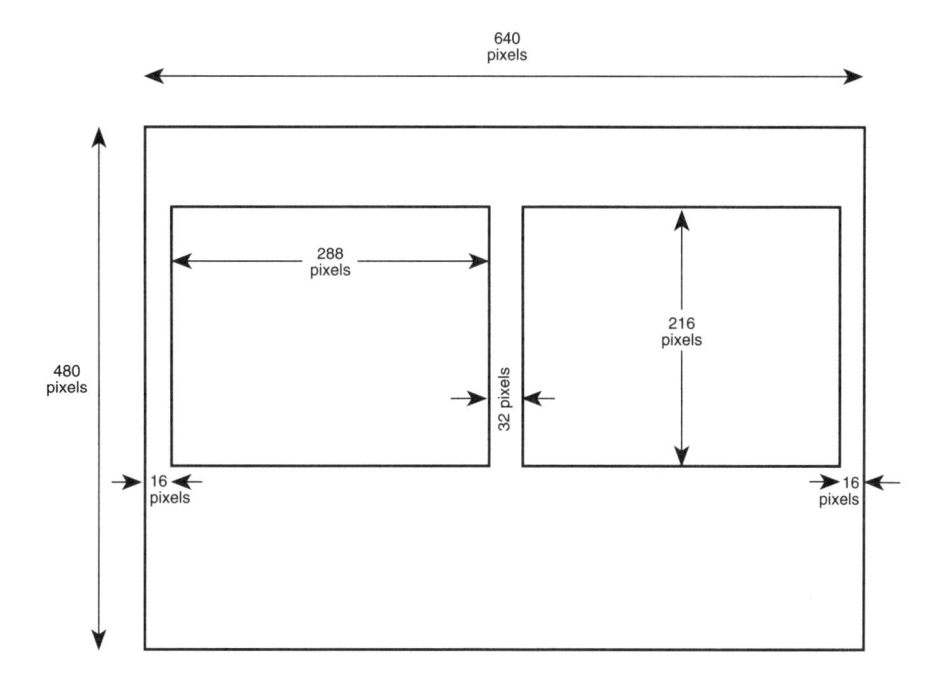

Figure 7.4

Specifications for stereo pair positioning on a 640x480 screen.

To view the images, use the freeware picture view provided, PICEM.EXE. To use PICEM, type

```
CD \QUE3D\3DPICS
PICEM
```

You will see a list of pictures. The stereo pairs begin with *str*. Select the one you want to view using the arrow keys, then press Enter. The images contained on this disk are 16-color VGA GIF images. They are viewable on a standard VGA display system. If you have a Macintosh, the images are still viewable, but you have to send them via modem to your Macintosh or use software that enables you to read PC floppy disks and transfer them that way. GIF is the *Graphics Interchange Format* made standard by CompuServe.

If you don't have a stereoscope or other viewing device, try to focus on the dot at the center of the screen until the images fuse into one. Some people find this technique easy, whereas others find it difficult. Just experiment and see if it works for you. With some practice, it's a nice way to view in stereo quickly. Remember that to make your eyes diverge is very uncomfortable. To avoid this, be sure you are using a monitor that is no more than 15 inches diagonal. Larger monitors result in larger images, which can be very difficult to resolve without a stereoscope.

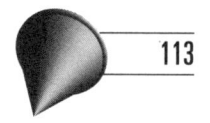

II USING THE COMPUTER FOR 3-D VISUALIZATION

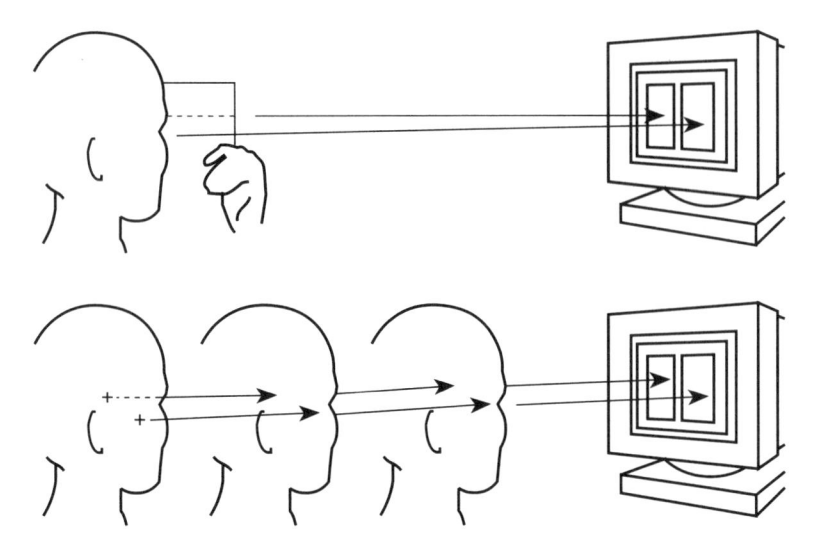

Figure 7.5

Free viewing of stereo pairs.

Figure 7.5 illustrates a method for free-viewing stereo pairs. Start by putting your face very close to the computer monitor. Then, while fixating on the same portion of each respective image with each eye, move your head away from the monitor very slowly. The pictures should resolve into a single "third" image in the center which is in 3-D. If this does not work, try holding a piece of cardboard between your eyes and repeating the same motion.

Drawing in Stereo

So, just how do you go about generating a stereo pair? Aside from taking a pair of photographs, having them developed, and scanning them, the easiest is way is by drawing one directly. When drawing stereo pairs, it is easiest to set the infinity plane, then separate the lines you draw by increasing amounts as you move forward. Included on the disk with this book is a program called STEREOD. Assuming you have installed the software properly (see the last page of this book if you have not yet installed the software), change into the STEREOD directory by typing

```
C:
CD \QUE3D\STEREOD
```

Run the program by typing

```
STEREOD
```

114

STEREO IMAGERY ON COMPUTER

You should see a screen that looks like figure 7.6.

Figure 7.6

The STEREOD start-up screen.

The left side of the screen is the icon bar and the right portion is the drawing area. The icons function as follows:

CLR—Clears the screen

DEMO—Runs a collection of sample images for testing

0 through 8—Sets the relative distance toward you the image is projected

EXIT—Quits the program

The right side of the screen is divided into two segments. The left half is the left-eye portion and the right half is the right-eye portion. You can draw only in the left-eye portion; the program automatically draws the right side for you. In the center, you see two dark gray lines. These are the image boundaries, and they are here only for illustrative purposes. Near the top at the center is a white dot. You can use this dot to help resolve images you create using one of the free-viewing methods.

Before drawing your own images, experiment with the built-in demos. Click the DEMO button. The screen should now look like figure 7.7.

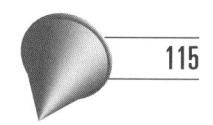

II USING THE COMPUTER FOR 3-D VISUALIZATION

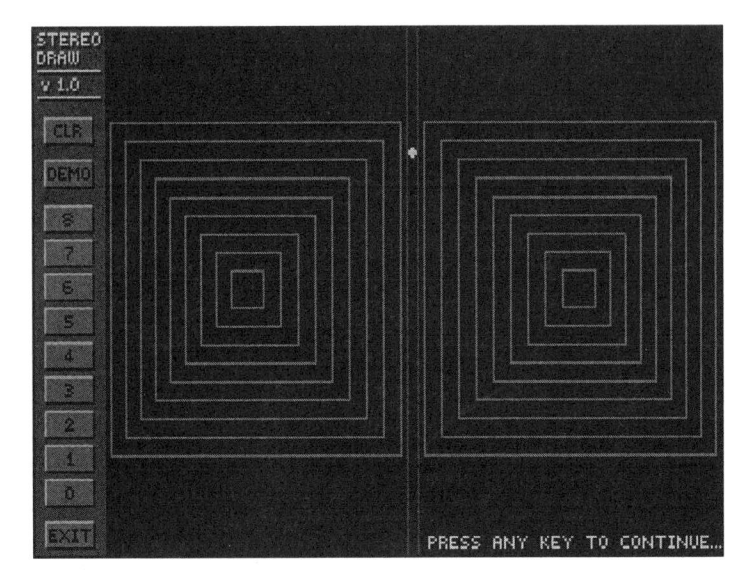

Figure 7.7

The first screen of DEMO.

Assuming you are using a stereoscope, adjust your position so that your head is approximately three feet from the screen. Now move your head from side to side. The image should look like a pyramid that is receding into the screen. If you are having trouble resolving the 3-D effect, try moving closer to or further from the screen. Move your head from side to side. After you have resolved the 3-D effect, press any key.

The pyramid should appear to come out of the screen toward you. Again, move your head from side to side to get the full effect. As I said in Chapter 6, if you cannot resolve the 3-D effect, you might be one of a small percentage of people who simply cannot resolve 3-D images, or you might be slightly color-blind. Now try to make your own 3-D images. Start by selecting the 0 parameter for reference. This selects equal separation of the lines. In other words, this is the infinity plane where no binocular separation (retinal disparity) occurs.

Draw a squiggle in the center of the screen. The screen should now look like figure 7.8.

Click the 8 button and draw a larger squiggle upward and to the left of your first squiggle. Then draw another squiggle downward and to the right of the reference point. You intentionally draw these second objects larger than the first to aid in the 3-D effect. Because

STEREO IMAGERY ON COMPUTER

they are closer to you, your brain thinks they should be larger. This is not definitive, of course, but it makes things easier to demonstrate.

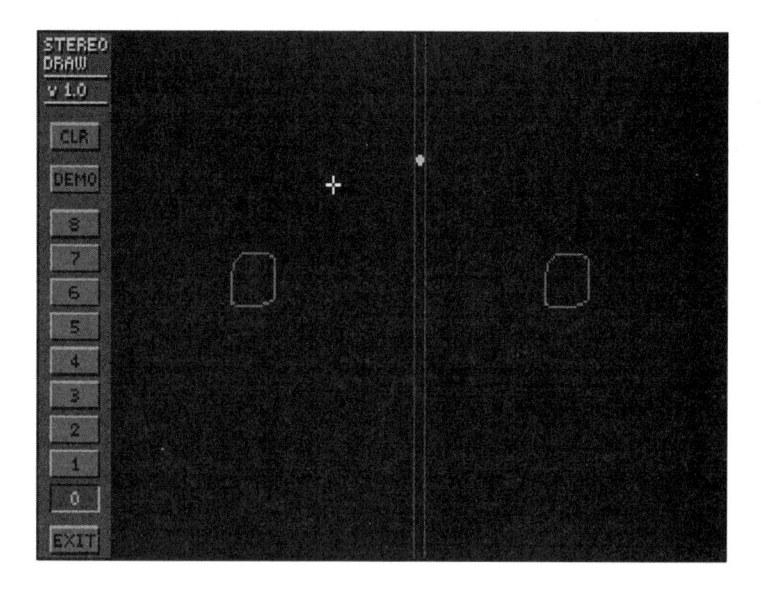

Figure 7.8
Setting the reference point.

Now look at your masterpiece. The top left squiggle should look like it is closer to you than the reference squiggle. Try other variations and see how dramatic an effect you can create. This time, try drawing while looking through a stereoscope. As you change screen depths, it appears as though you can draw under and over previously drawn lines. This type of program has no real use, but it is an interesting way to explore how stereo images work. After a little practice with STEREOD, you will find that working with normal 3-D programs and generating stereo pairs is a snap!

Hardware Stereo Viewing Devices

So far, this chapter has dealt with viewing a side-by-side pair of images. The stereo viewing technique depends on some method of separation of the images so that only one image is seen by each eye. Then, the brain takes over and performs the fusing. Since the development of 3-D imagery on a computer, researchers have attempted to eliminate the problems associated with pair viewing, such as ghosting and uncomfortable viewing apparatuses.

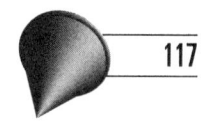

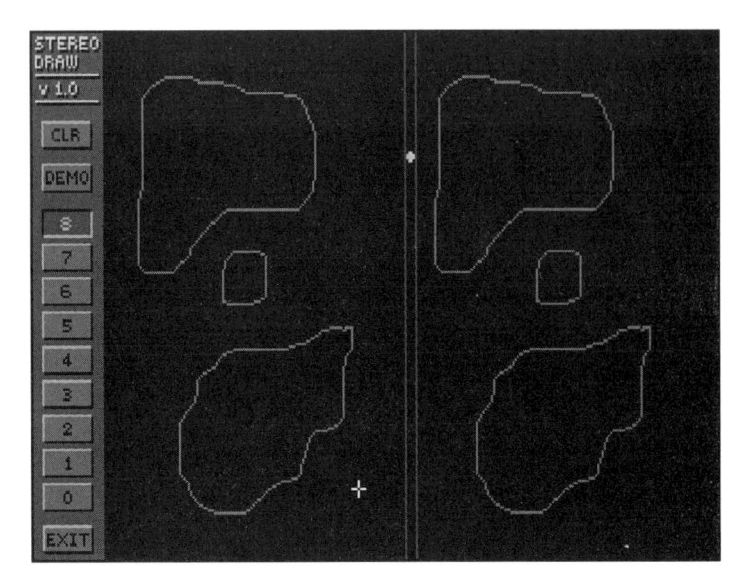

Figure 7.9

Your first stereo image.

LCD Shutter Glasses

Another problem encountered is the limited size of the images. Wouldn't it be nice if you could see a full-screen image? Well, you can with the proper device. This device has several forms, but the most economical variation is the LCD shutter. Several versions are available, including one that was provided by Sega for use with its early game systems. These inexpensive glasses can be hardware-modified to work with an IBM-compatible PC. Although no longer available from Sega, they can still be acquired through the hobbyist market.

The system works by taking each image of the stereo pair and storing it in a separate screen buffer. This requires a graphics system with enough video memory to hold two images of the desired resolution and color depth and a mechanism for very quickly switching between the graphics pages. On the IBM-compatible VGA (Video Graphics Array) system, this is limited to 640×480 in 16 colors. With special modifications to newer technologies called SuperVGA, resolutions of up to 800×600 in 256 colors are possible.

Instead of viewing both images simultaneously, one image is displayed at a time and the electronic shutter closes over the unused eye. This way, the left eye sees the left image and the right eye sees only the right image. This must all happen very quickly. Because monitors typically refresh at 60Hz, each eye sees its respective image 30 times a second. This is fast enough for the persistence of vision to be maintained so that the image appears continuous. If the frames were not refreshed fast enough, flicker would occur.

StereoGraphics Crystal Eyes

One of the leaders in the 3-D vision field is StereoGraphics Corporation. StereoGraphics makes a system which works similarly to the LCD shutters, but on a much higher level. The shutters are controlled via infrared signal rather than clumsy wires, and dedicated systems are built which support very high resolution and color depths. The Crystal Eyes systems are used primarily for scientific analysis and presentation purposes. Although expensive for the hobbyist, there are no competitors in the pure 3-D projection arena. Exploration is also being done with systems such as Crystal Eyes to support real-time 3-D applications in virtual reality.

Summary

Although usually not available in a full-screen format, stereo pairs on the computer screen offer advantages over anaglyphs in that they retain all of their color. A simple stereoscope such as the VCH reflecting stereoscope is useful in viewing on-screen stereo pairs. Without a stereoscope, relaxed viewing or free-viewing is acceptable as an alternative method.

Virtually all 3-D programs have the ability to generate stereo pairs, even if it is not an automatic function of the program. All you need is two camera locations and some creativity. Special effects such as hyper-stereo and hypo-stereo are easily generated by manipulating the camera positions and viewing parameters. Stereo animations are generated as easily as stills. Some programs like Virtual Reality Labs' Vistapro have a built-in stereo generator. This makes the production of real 3-D fly-throughs easy.

With special hardware systems such as LCD shutters and the StereoGraphics Corporation Crystal Eyes product, the ultimate in 3-D viewing is possible. By eliminating the problems associated with pair viewing on a computer screen, greater 3-D effects are transmitted directly to the brain. The more realistic the 3-D effect, the easier it is to escape into our computer world.

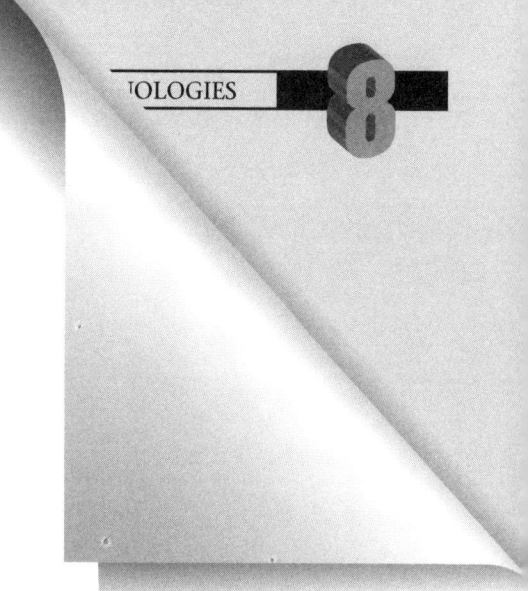

Other 3-D Technologies

Fractals

Fractal geometry is a relatively new branch of mathematics which deals in objects which have fractional dimension. This means that they lie outside the plane of real-number mathematics. Fractals are used to describe naturally occurring objects. Clouds, rocks, mountains, and even the texture of skin can be described with a complex set of mathematical equations. Let's take a look at this fascinating world, and particularly at 3-D applications of fractals.

Background and History

The principal attribute of fractals (a derivative of the Latin word *frangere*, which means *to break*, and *fractus*, which means *fragmented*) is that they appear irregular or fragmented when compared to objects from Euclidean geometry, such as lines (one dimension), planes (two dimensions), and spheres (three dimensions). Another unique feature is that fractals continue to appear fragmented as they are scaled up. If you zoom into the side of a rectangle, it becomes a very simple object—a line.

II USING THE COMPUTER FOR 3-D VISUALIZATION

No matter how close you zoom into a fractal, it retains its self-similarity, complexity, and irregular nature. This infinite irregularity is what makes fractals ideal for defining seemingly nonsymmetric natural shapes such as mountains and trees.

Before we investigate complex fractals, take a look at the simplest of all fractals, the Cantor bar. This apparently obvious but until recently undefined fractal was first proposed by the famous 19th-century mathematician Georg Cantor. Imagine a long, straight line. Divide that line into three equal-length pieces. Now remove the center piece. Perform this same operation with the two remaining pieces so that four are left. Do it again until eight remain (fig. 8.1). If this process is continued into infinity, our previously defined conditions are met. That is, each piece retains the complexity of the original and is self-similar.

Figure 8.1

The Cantor bar.

Although this shape is not of fractal dimension, it illustrates the basic principle. There are other illustrative examples. An equilateral triangle, for example, can be divided into three completely similar but smaller triangles. Each of these triangles can again be divided into three more, and so on. Regardless of how many times they are divided, the result still resembles the original. There is no mathematical end to the division.

Another more complex (philosophically, anyway) example is time. Any specific unit of time can be divided into smaller units. These smaller units are identical in composition to the first. A second is mathematically similar to a minute, it just doesn't last as long.

OTHER 3-D TECHNOLOGIES

However, time theory is not easily pursued with computer graphics, so it is beyond our scope here.

According to Benoit Mandelbrot, the modern father of fractal geometry and Fellow at IBM's Watson Research Institute, the equation which describes a fractal must have an imaginary dimension. These sets of numbers appear to fill the space between normal dimensional objects. You might remember this from high school math as the symbol *i* or the square root of –1. These fractal sets of numbers are called *nonlinear sets* because they vary slightly over the entire group. This means that a number early in the set may bear no immediate resemblance to numbers which appear later in the set, but numbers close together remain similar.

Many other types of fractals are commonly accepted which do not have imaginary components. These are called *linear sets*. Modern fractal theorists argue over the proper use of the word *fractal*. The subject of argument is which sets of numbers are to be included under this term, because so many different theories are being developed simultaneously. For now, we won't be concerned with cognitive dissension in the mathematical community.

Fractals really took off in 1967, when Mandelbrot published a paper that used mathematics to describe the coast of England. It was shown that the closer you zoomed into the map, the more accurate it got, rather than the opposite. Mandelbrot continued his research and published many papers on the subject. In 1975, he published his theory of fractal geometry. Many other mathematicians quickly followed suit. Before long, the most famous of all sets, the Mandelbrot set, was established (see fig. 8.2). In August 1985, *Scientific American* magazine presented the public with a Mandelbrot fractal on its cover. Today, the Mandelbrot set forms the basis for learning and research into fractal space.

With the growth in computer graphics applications, a new method for visualizing fractal space emerged. By assigning different colors to the elements of a two-dimensional table of numbers, the first color fractal was formed. Soon afterward, these elaborate computer images were the basis for fractal exploration. Computer images provided a way for humans to see a part of their world they had never even imagined before. When the element of three dimensions was added, scientists noticed the similarity between certain fractal

II USING THE COMPUTER FOR 3-D VISUALIZATION

sets and the real world. Suddenly, computer-generated trees, mountains, and oceans were created. Seemingly random cloud formations took on a newfound regularity when generated from equations.

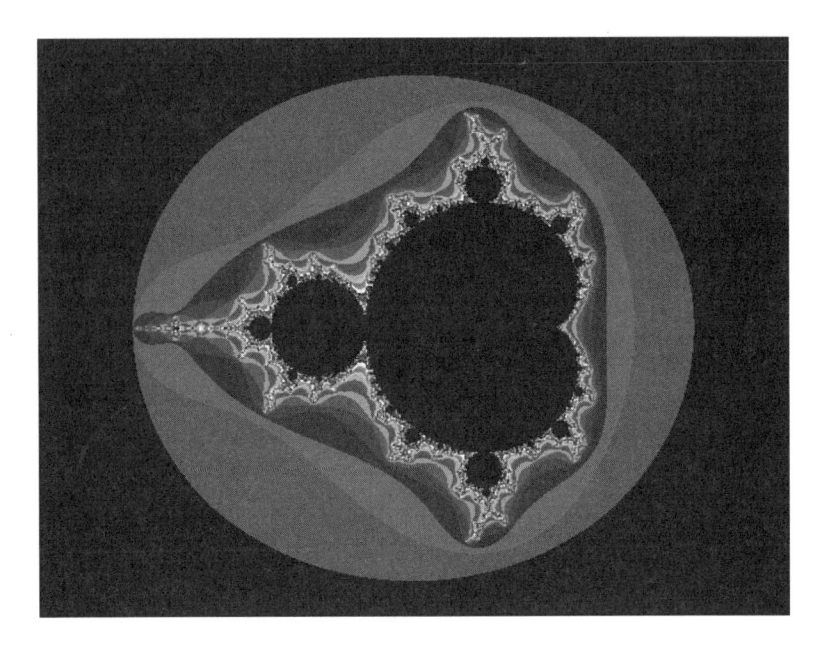

Figure 8.2

The Mandelbrot set.

Two issues confront the fractal scientist. The first is the easy one: how to create a realistic image from mathematics through application of computer graphics. The second is more difficult: how to fit mathematical equations to existing natural phenomena. It is one thing to create a realistic mountain from fractals, but indeed another to fit the proper equations to describe El Capitan in the south of Yosemite. This use of fractals to describe natural phenomena combined with the projection of the results into three dimensions is where we will focus much of our fractal attention in this book.

Fractal Technology for Real-Life Simulations

Plotting a shoreline is a two-dimensional process. If you were to modify the Cantor bar theory by taking the middle piece and, instead of removing it (as in line B_1), altering its angle and then

OTHER 3-D TECHNOLOGIES

realigning the end pieces with the angled centerpiece (as in line B_2), you could simulate a shoreline (see fig. 8.3). The closer you get to the shore, the more pieces the line can be broken into and the more accurate it becomes.

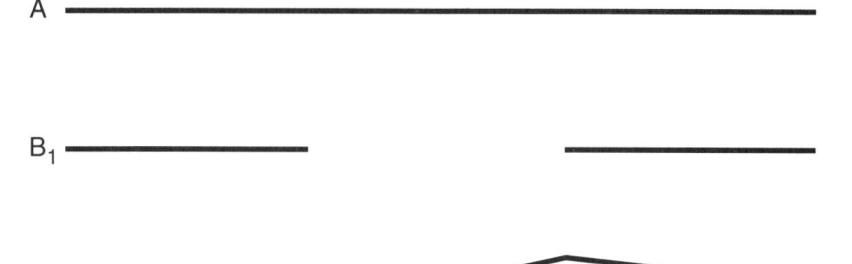

A ─────────────────────────

B₁ ────────   ────────

B₂ ──────────╲╱──────────────

Figure 8.3
A modified Cantor bar.

This is not the actual technique for calculating shorelines, but it serves as a practical example. At some point of magnification, the shoreline is constantly changing. Therefore, if the data set used to calculate the shore is a set of primary points (rocky crags, major inlets and bays, and so on), the points between can be randomly or fractally calculated so that a realistic shoreline is approximated. This brings up an interesting question, "How accurate can this possibly be?"

There is an old story about differential calculus which bears repeating. One day, a student was having a difficult time understanding the theory of limits. The teacher of mathematics had just asked this question of the class: If you take a line and cut it in half, then cut it in half again, and then again, and repeat this procedure an infinite number of times, will the length of the line ever reach zero? The student was very logical and concluded that no matter how short the line got, half of it would always remain. Wrong! the teacher exclaimed. With this, the teacher asked the student to go to the front of the room. He then asked him to face the water fountain. He asked the student to go halfway to the fountain, then halfway again and halfway again. He asked if the student if he could get a drink of water. No, said the student, it is too far away. This process was repeated until the student's belly was up against the water fountain. "Are you there yet?" asked the teacher. "Yes, for all practical intents and purposes," replied the student.

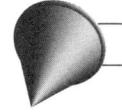

The point of this story is that when dealing in real-world mapping and simulations, an exact science is not necessary. Just as the student got close enough to perform the requested task, taking a drink, the measurements of our shoreline are close enough to perform mapping, erosion analysis, and beach management. By randomly varying the angles of displacement but maintaining the hard data, realistic shorelines are created. Is our random angular alteration any more predictable or any less precise than that created by the lapping waves of the ocean?

To get a mental picture of how to map the real world in three dimensions, try the following. Imagine a piece of paper in the shape of a triangle. Now, draw lines from all three points to the center. Take this center point and raise it to a specified altitude. Repeat this process by drawing lines on the remaining triangles. Again, raise them to an altitude slightly less than the first. If this process is repeated over and over, you soon have what looks like a crumpled piece of paper, but its irregular surface looks like a jagged mountain. If you assign computer pixels to these elevations and then color them according to elevation using blue for the lower elevations; green, gray, and brown for the middle; and white for the top, a fractal landscape appears.

By performing this operation with predefined elevation data sets, the computer can be programmed to "draw" mountains that we already know a great deal about. To generate random mountains, we merely have to seed our program with random data rather than measured data. Thus, we address the same issues that confront the fractal scientist—the generation of new terrain and the understanding of existing terrain—with startling accuracy.

There are many uses for this technology. For educational purposes, we can add waves to the water, put lakes and rivers where none existed before, change the snow level, and repopulate our depleted forests. Artists use it for generating realistic scenery. Game developers generate backgrounds. Meteorologists create photo-realistic cloud maps. Space explorers can generate realistic models of distant worlds from data gathered on various missions.

How far will it go? As more and more of our planet is explored and measured, the data sets will become increasingly more accurate.

OTHER 3-D TECHNOLOGIES

After a major earthquake or volcanic eruption, the data sets are updated. It is not known exactly how the two will work in tandem, but it is commonly accepted in the scientific community that chaos theory (the theory of how and why seemingly random occurrences happen) and fractal geometry (mathematics explaining the occurrences after they happen) together will go a long way toward predicting natural disasters. By studying *before* and *after* scenarios, scientists hope to gather enough information to start piecing together the complex puzzles of the world in which we live.

Virtual Reality

One of the newest frontiers being explored by graphics researchers is virtual reality. VR is a topic for entire books; however, a basic understanding is helpful when you deal with the world of 3-D. In simple terms, VR can be thought of as real-time 3-D. Although there is more to VR than just moving images, it is the 3-D imaging that provides the stage on which VR enthusiasts play.

Background and History

At first, this sounds like a good section title, but deeper thought reveals its ludicrous nature. How can we discuss the history of a subject that is only a few years old? Easy: We make it up!

Let's begin with a basic understanding of what Virtual Reality means. If this is the third book you've read on VR, it will probably be the third definition you have heard. It is easiest to look individually at the words. Start with *virtual*. In computer terminology, when we speak of *virtual memory*, we are referring to something that is not real. Virtual memory is disk space that "acts" like memory to the computer program trying to use it. So, something that is virtual is something that is not really what it claims, but for all intents and purposes "appears" to be.

Reality is a totally different concept. It means many things to many people. For psychological and philosophical reasons, let's not dig into it too much here, but define it to mean the "real" world. The real world includes objects in three dimensions. It means travel in those same three dimensions. It means the existence of our five basic senses. It means emotions and the human existence.

So what then is *virtual reality*? It is the perception of reality where none exists. Simple, huh? Let's look deeper. The last time you were at the movies, weren't you completely caught up in the story to the point where you had to come back to your world when the movie was over? This is a mild form of virtual reality. For a while there, you actually thought you were in the movie. Of course, your sensual involvement was limited. Without the smell, taste, and touch sensations, you are bound by what you can see and hear. It happens that these senses, when affected strongly, are enough to allow your brain to escape your own world and enter another. When was the last time you found yourself wanting to smell something you saw in a movie? Your involvement through sight and sound is so strong that your brain fills in the gaps.

VR on a Computer

Virtual reality on the computer usually refers to the use of a computer as a controlling device in a virtual reality environment. There are several computer programs that claim to be VR applications that are nothing more than fast 3-D programs. There is some resemblance to real-world movement, but without a real stretch of your imagination, they are just fun and games and are jumping on the VR bandwagon to generate marketing hype.

Real involvement in a virtual world must embrace a concept known as *immersion*. Immersion means simply that you are totally involved in the world you are experiencing. If you really feel like you are flying when you play a flight simulator, then it is a form of VR. If you just feel like it is a really neat 3-D game, then the excitement may be there, but it isn't VR.

VR for VR's Sake

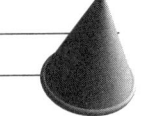

It is logical for computer enthusiasts to explore the VR world with 3-D graphics and simulations. But will they replace the sensation you get when chomping into a hot chocolate chip cookie? Probably not for a while. The easiest road to follow is the "let's make this new technology look like something we already know" road.

Remember TV commercials in the 60s? They were radio jingles with moving pictures in front. Now, television and video have developed into a medium all their own. The same will happen with VR; but for now, we are limited to totally noncreative types who are trying to make a buck by making our computer screens look like a TV set. The real VR pioneers are exploring new senses.

Making "Sense" of It All

There have been numerous books and movies in which an investigator working on a murder claimed to have access to a supposed "sixth" sense. Although the topic of heated discussion, there seems no disagreement in the VR world that more than five senses exist and can be manipulated. Among candidates for the official sixth sense are gravity and other forces, proprioception (like the perception of balance), and the changes we feel when things become chemically unbalanced in our systems. These and other sensory receptors are being explored by researchers in an effort to control as much of our life in a virtual sense as possible.

Input and Output

You can find a detailed discussion in many books about virtual reality, but our discussion would not be complete without some reference to the various input devices that are used to control virtual worlds. These include gloves that allow manipulation through little sensors on fingertips and along the hand structure, various types of motion detectors that fit on our bodies, and even muscle contraction sensors that tell when our eyes change direction. This is important to the computer VR world because through the use of a computer, we are able to do something movies will never do in their traditional form: interact with them. Watching a world unfold in front of you on a large screen is a nice experience. However, VR, by our own definition, must allow us to interact with it because we are able to interact with our own reality. Interactive movies are coming, though!

Output devices are just as important as input devices. The obvious choice is a display device for our eyes and speakers for our ears. But what do we do about smell, taste, and the other senses? All the senses must be included for complete virtual reality. All of us have had dreams that were so real we pinched ourselves during the dream to see if it was real. As long as an action can take place that reminds us that not everything is real, the scene is not complete.

With VR display technology improving, it won't be long before the scene we see in front of our eyes is as complete as the real world, visually. Audio is already at realistic quality. But the other senses will have to wait. A complete smell regenerator is a way off. Electronic stimulus to represent touch exists, but is a long way from being realistic. Tastes can be reproduced, but the task of delivering the message to our tongues is a tricky one. Balance, chemical changes, and any other sixth senses that are generated are still being explored. But that brings us back to the most powerful tool we have for VR, our eyes.

Vision—specifically 3-D vision—is one of the most powerful influences on how we feel. Many other senses are affected by what our brain creates as a result of what we see or think we see. It is possible to generate motion sickness in a person who isn't moving at all. Just sit him in front of an OmniMax movie, and his brain will think he is there and begin the processes of compensation for the sensations he sees. The right visual image of a freshly-baked cookie or pie can make our mouths water, even with no odor present. We react to what we see more strongly than from any other input.

Sound is also important, but not as important as sight. (This is unless we are speaking of blind people. They quite often have acute hearing because it is the primary tool by which they "see" the world around them.) Sounds are logged into our memories and can later trigger emotional responses in an instant. Watch a mother's reaction when she hears a baby cry. What is it that makes certain voices "familiar"? Volume, pitch, language, and intensity all contribute to what we interpret when we hear a sound. If VR units of the future can understand and re-create our real world of sounds, they will go a long way toward being effective.

So where does all of this lead us? Do we really want VR? Here's a sample scenario to explore for a moment:

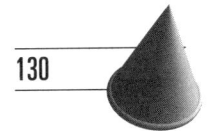

OTHER 3-D TECHNOLOGIES

> *You are walking down a dark street in London on a typically cool, foggy evening. The streetlights shimmer a faded yellow above you and the distant sounds of bar-room jocularity break the night still, if only slightly. Suddenly, a loud screeching sound explodes in the night and you turn to see an out-of-control car careening directly toward you. You jump aside and land against the wall of a building in a pile of rubbish tossed out by a local restaurant. You get up, dust yourself off, and notice that the foul stench of rotting fish has worked its way into your topcoat. Reaching into your pocket, you find a slimy, old banana peel. You quickly fling it down, wiping your hand off on your trouser leg. As you continue on your journey, you are left with a feeling that this is just like a scene from a movie. You find yourself asking, "Is this really happening to me?"*

Just think for a moment. What if you couldn't tell? What if VR technology was so advanced that there was absolutely no way to distinguish reality from fantasy? Isn't that the goal of VR researchers, to as closely as possible re-create a realistic situation?

Applications

The answer is simply, no. The real goal of most VR research is to find ways to duplicate real-life situations in such a way that they are useful to us. For example, surgical medicine benefits greatly from having realistic training grounds. Exploring the internal workings of the human body is done best when done on a non-human! Actual surgical procedures could be practiced until near perfection was imminent before encountering the real patient. VR is a good tool for exploring any world that is difficult to explore in real life.

The sciences are well-served by 3-D and VR exploration. Chemical molecules that are too small to see with the naked eye or even microscopes are easy to model and manipulate with 3-D and VR tools. This ability enables scientists to solve problems that affect the world on a much larger scale. There is some talk of using VR mechanisms to explore the world of infectious diseases. Physicists use holographic VR worlds to explore subatomic particles and the atomic-sized world in general. Holography in itself is a major contributor to the world of VR.

Education at all levels is greatly enhanced by the use of simulation and real-world re-creation. Imagine a place where children not only read and listen, but also interact with the world they are learning about. They could explore the seas, climb the highest mountains, and see faraway lands. They could learn to deal with obstacles that impede their progress along the way. They could learn geometry and trigonometry from a complete, three dimensional point of view.

One of the biggest obstacles in learning 3-D computer systems today is that we have no experience in thinking in 3-D. This is a very strange concept because we live in a 3-D world, but it is true. The translation of three dimensions into two (our computer screen or book pages) leaves many questions unanswered to a student with little or no knowledge of complex matrix algebra. But with VR, the translation process can be eliminated. Three-dimensional worlds will appear exactly as they really exist, so the brain will not have to make that translation.

Summary

Fractal technology and virtual reality are just two areas in which three-dimensional manipulation is being applied to help us understand the world in which we live. Fractals can be used to explore areas of mathematical space that we never knew existed. They can also be used to represent the world we think we know so much about. When applied through computer graphics technology, fractal space is a beautiful as well as wondrous thing. Much contemporary art is based on fractals and chaos. When fractal technology is applied in three dimensions to data we can measure, our world suddenly grows up around us. Software programs such as Vistapro from Virtual Reality Laboratories (a demo of which is included with this book) allow us to manipulate fractal landscapes with a startling degree of realism. Fractals and the computer go hand in hand as tools for understanding our future.

After we create our world, we have a need to explore it. Virtual reality research is providing the tools necessary in this quest. 3-D computer systems that operate in real time provide the visual information delivery platform. Audio tracks synchronized with the computer movies add to the stimulus. Interactive technologies allow us to explore *immersion*, the key to VR systems. As we get further involved with these imaginary worlds, better and better tools are necessary to stimulate all the senses to provide a complete simulation. How far will it all go? No one knows for sure, but the next time you find you have to ask the question, "Is this real?", you might be closer than you think.

Part III

3-D Computer Applications

3-D Gaming—Wolfenstein 3-D

As has been mentioned in previous chapters, the biggest advances in new technology are usually in areas that receive the most funding. This is because of the tremendous research and development costs involved. Computer games, multimedia, and motion pictures are the biggest investment cash resources available to the computer graphics marketplace—and specifically, the 3-D marketplace. This book includes one of the most advanced computer games as an example of how 3-D is being used for gaming: Wolfenstein 3-D.

Technology

To gain maximum performance in computer graphics, most games are written in a very fast language, such as C, with critical subroutines and internal loops optimized at the machine level in Assembly language. This is the case with Wolfenstein 3-D, which ensures that the game takes full advantage of whatever processor your computer has.

III 3-D COMPUTER APPLICATIONS

Although there are many other virtual reality-style games out there, most are limited to primitive polygon graphics. A simple polygon is very fast to draw and makes for fast gaming when real-time changes in 3-D are required. However, the technicians at ID Software have created a system that allows textures to be applied to the 3-D walls, resulting in a more realistic effect than in any other game. The result is that games can be designed that allow details down to the individual pixel level.

Sound is also an important aspect of contemporary gaming. Life-like sound effects must share processing time with the graphics engine. If extremely well-written code is not used, timing problems and smoothness issues might arise. By using the DMA (direct memory access) modes of sound cards, you can avoid most of these problems.

There are limitations to the core program, however. For one, walls can be placed only at 90-degree angles to each other. Walls must always be square and of the same thickness. Floors and ceilings do not have the same textured detail as the walls, but this is not a noticeable limitation. The engineers at ID are always working on new technology, however, and promise a fully-textured room for future releases.

As you play Wolfenstein 3-D, be careful! The super-fast scrolling has been known to cause motion sickness in an average of 5 percent of its players! If you start to feel queasy, use the keyboard rather than the mouse and slow down a little. If you like a good amusement ride, the turbulence of virtual reality simulation won't phase you in the least.

The Story So Far...(from the Wolfenstein Player's Manual)

You're William J. "BJ" Blakowicz, the Allies' bad boy of espionage and a terminal action seeker.

Your mission was to infiltrate the Nazi fortress Castle Hollehammer and find the plans for Operation Eisenfaust (Iron Fist), the Nazi blueprint for building the perfect army. Rumors are that deep within Castle Hollehammer the diabolical Dr. Schabbs has perfected

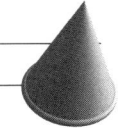

3-D GAMING—WOLFENSTEIN 3-D

a technique for building a fierce army from the bodies of the dead. It's so far removed from reality that it would seem silly if it wasn't so sick. But what if it were true?

You never got a chance to find out! Captured in your attempt to grab the secret plans, you were taken to the Nazi prison, Wolfenstein, for questioning and eventual execution. For 12 long days, you've been imprisoned beneath the castle fortress. Just beyond your cell door sits a lone, thick-necked Nazi guard. He assisted an SS dentist/mechanic in an attempt to jump-start your tonsils earlier this morning.

You're at your breaking point! Quivering on the floor you beg for medical assistance in return for information. His face hints a smug grin of victory as he reaches for his keys. He opens the door, the tumblers in the lock echo through the corridors, and the door squeaks open. HIS MISTAKE!

A single kick to his knee sends him to the floor. Giving him your version of the victory sign, you grab his knife and quickly finish the job. You stand over the guard's fallen body, grabbing frantically for his gun. You're not sure if the other guards heard his muffled scream. Deep in the belly of a Nazi dungeon, you must escape. This desperate act has sealed your fate—get out or die trying.

Starting the Game

Before you can play Wolfenstein 3-D, you must install the software as described on the disk installation page at the end of this book. After you have done so, go to the WOLF3D directory by typing the following:

```
C:
CD\QUE3D\WOLF3D
```

To start the game, type

```
WOLF3D
```

You see a system status screen, a copyright notice, then the official start-up screen, as seen in figure 9.1.

Press a key again and you are at the options screen. Before you actually play the game, you must decide how brave you are. Select New Game from the options screen. You see the following choices:

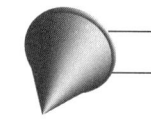

139

III 3-D COMPUTER APPLICATIONS

- Can I play, Daddy? (This selection is for novices or the basically chicken-hearted.)
- Don't hurt me (Good for first-timers).
- Bring 'em on (For most avid game players).
- I am Death incarnate (For the *really* bold)!

Figure 9.1

The Wolfenstein 3-D start-up screen.

Each level is increasingly more difficult, adding more bad guys and decreasing the damage you can take before succumbing to the enemy. After you make your selection, the game begins.

Movement

The easiest way to move around the game is with a mouse. You push the mouse forward to go forward, backward to move backward, and side to side to turn left and right. You can move basically as fast as you can move the mouse. If you do not have a mouse, you can use the arrow keys. To move faster, hold down right-Shift and use the arrows. To slide sideways, use right-Alt and the left and right arrows.

Arms

There are several different weapons available to you. You begin with the knife and a pistol. Buried in the maze are a machine gun and a chain gun. The machine gun and chain gun are necessary to defeat some of the tougher foes. You can use the knife if you are out of ammunition, but it is best to use the guns when possible. To switch between weapons, press the following keys:

    1—Knife

    2—Pistol

    3—Machine gun

    4—Chain gun

If you press 3 or 4 before you find the machine gun or chain gun, it has no effect.

Killing the Enemy

To use your weapon, point it toward your opponent and press the Ctrl key. If you hold down the Ctrl key, your gun fires continuously; however, you are likely to run out of ammo quickly. Pressing the left button on the mouse has the same effect. The closer you are to the enemy, the more deadly your shot is. But so is his! Don't be afraid to shoot him in the back. There is no room for fair play in Wolfenstein.

Doors

To open doors and elevators, press the Spacebar. If you are using a three-button mouse, you can use the middle button to perform the same function. When you get close to a door, just press the Spacebar and it opens. There are walls within the castle that you can open like doors to reveal hidden rooms and passageways. There are also several doors which require special keys (usually found in treasure rooms). When you have the key, the door opens with the Spacebar just like other doors. If a door won't open for you, it probably needs a key—so go looking for one.

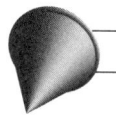

III 3-D COMPUTER APPLICATIONS

Stuff

To pick up an object in the various rooms throughout the dungeon, simply walk over it. The items you might find useful are

- Healing/Food: Little trays of food and first-aid kits are the strongest food and healing supplements (10% and 25%, respectively). You can also gather some strength by eating the dog food. Don't be shy! If your health is 100%, picking up food has no effect.

> **Tip:** If you have less than 10% health, you can also get a little nourishment from the pools of swill on the floor throughout the dungeon.

- Killing: Ammo is in little blue boxes left behind by dead Nazis. You should also keep your eyes open for the machine gun and the chain gun.

- Treasure: As in any game, the object is to stay alive and gather points. Various objects relinquish different amounts of points. They are

    Crown: 5000 points

    Chest: 1000 points

    Chalice: 500 points

    Cross: 100 points

- Special items: There are keys that open special doors scattered throughout. Also be on the lookout for little faces, which are extra life-givers. They can be worth one life, full health, or full ammo.

The Next Floor

Each level of the game contains an elevator that will send you to the next floor. Press the Spacebar to open the elevator door, then press the Spacebar again inside to go up. There is no going back after you go to the next level. There are nine levels plus a special

3-D GAMING—WOLFENSTEIN 3-D

secret level in each episode of the game. You get only one episode with this special version of the game. If you check with the references in Appendix A, however, you can get five more exciting episodes.

The following is a summary of the keys used in Wolfenstein 3-D and what they do:

Key	Action
F1	Help
Pause	Pause
Esc	Options
F2	Save game
F3	Load game
F4	Sound toggle
F5	View
F6	Control
F7	End game
F8	Quick save
F9	Quick load
F10	Quit
1	Knife
2	Pistol
3	Machine gun
4	Chain gun
Up Arrow	Move forward
Down Arrow	Move backward
Left Arrow	Turn left
Right Arrow	Turn right
Shift+Up arrow	Run forward
Shift+Down arrow	Run backward

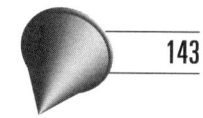

continues

III 3-D COMPUTER APPLICATIONS

Key	Action
Shift+Left arrow	Fast left turn
Shift+Right arrow	Fast right turn
Alt+Left arrow	Strafe left
Alt+Right arrow	Strafe right
Ctrl	Shoot
Spacebar	Open doors

The Status Screen

At the bottom of the playing screen is a status bar. This information is useful while you are moving through the game. Figure 9.2 shows a typical game screen.

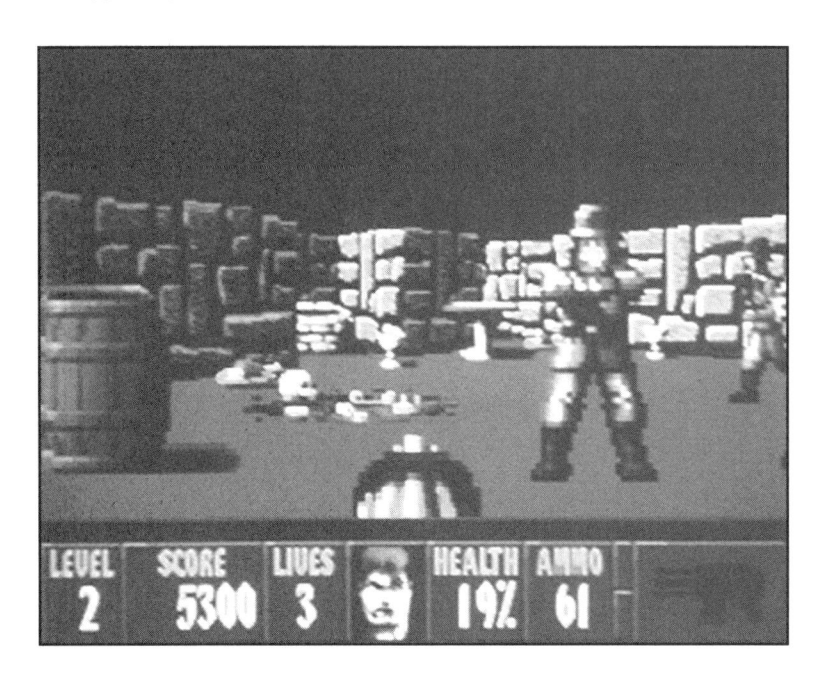

Figure 9.2

A typical scene from the game, including the status bar.

At the far left is the level indicator. This tells you which level you are on. There are nine levels per episode and an additional secret level.

To the right of the level indicator is the score. Each 40,000 points gives you an extra life, so gobble up those treasures. In addition, you get special points for getting through each level in record time with no hits and finding all secret doors.

The LIVES indicator tells you how many lives you have left. Each time you die, you are returned to the beginning of the current level with only your knife and pistol with eight shots. You also lose any extra points you have attained on that level by gathering treasures. Any Nazis you have killed come back to life.

Your health is indicated by both a percentage counter and a pictogram. If the face in the middle of the screen (yours!) gets to be bloody and drooping, look for some food—fast!

AMMO is the number of shots you have left. The maximum you can carry around at any time is 99. Remember that if you hold down the Ctrl key or mouse button, you fire continuously, which is more effective but uses up ammunition faster.

The two little rectangles to the right of the AMMO indicator are the key holders. If you have either or both keys, they appear in these areas.

At the far right is the current weapon indicator. Make sure you know which weapon you have selected before using it. It makes no sense to strafe with a knife!

After each level is completed, you see a summary screen that tells you how you fared on the previous level. Ratios are calculated for hidden rooms located, kills, and treasure found. Each 100% result gives you 10,000 extra points. Also, if you beat the predetermined PAR times for each level (the speed at which you completed it), you get extra bonus points.

Bad Guys

Episode one is a relatively simple introduction to the game system. In this episode, you encounter brown-suited guards. They are easy to kill and usually one shot will do. There are also blue-suited, bullet-proof-vested SS members. They are a little more difficult to kill, but go down fairly easily. There are German shepherd dogs scattered throughout the dungeon to guard special rooms. If you don't shoot first, they'll go for your throat!

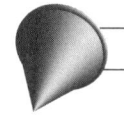

At level nine, you encounter Hans, the big boss. Be sure to have plenty of firepower and the chain gun if you want to have any chance of defeating him.

Hints

Hint 1: Don't just rush into a room. You have a better chance if you lay back and look around slowly.

Hint 2: Use the mouse for movement and the Spacebar for opening doors. This is the fastest way to get around. You must learn to be quick to get high scores and survive.

Hint 3: Use Quick Save often! Before you enter a room, you can press F8 for a quick save; then if you die, you can restart the game in the place it was before you went in.

Hint 4: Don't strafe unless it is needed. You will need to conserve ammo to get to the higher levels.

Hint 5: Look for the hidden rooms at every level. They almost always contain extra booty, and because you get an extra life for every 40,000 points, you can use all the treasures you can find.

Hint 6: The *M*, *L*, and *I* keys. If you are desperate, press the *M*, *L*, and *I* keys for full ammo and health. Unfortunately, your score goes to zero and 10 minutes are added to your time. But it is a nice way to escape total disaster.

Summary

3-D graphics are everywhere, but the most exciting new areas are in entertainment. Wolfenstein 3-D is a great example of how 3-D graphics are enhancing the way we entertain ourselves in the information age. Future technologies will enhance the speed, graphic quality, and overall effect of the games. With faster computers, higher-resolution graphics, and better programs, we may soon be able to jump right into the world of virtual reality!

3-D GAMING—WOLFENSTEIN 3-D

Figure 9.3

The Big Boss of episode 1.

Although the movement in this game is really only two-dimensional (did you notice that you cannot move up and down, only left, right, in, and out?), three-dimensional engines are in the works. Keep in touch with Apogee and other game manufacturers. You won't want to miss out on this exciting new medium for entertainment.

Hands-on with Vistapro

Installing the Software on Your System

Welcome to the world of Vistapro fractal landscape software. If you haven't read Chapter 8, now might be a good time to do so. It provides a basic overview of fractal theory and how it is applied to 3-D landscapes such as those generated by Vistapro. It will be easier for you to follow along with the tutorials in this chapter if you have a basic understanding of what we are doing. If you looked down at a square region of the Earth's surface from very high up, it would look flat. But if you divided that square into a grid, every point on that grid would have a specific elevation. Those elevation points are arranged into an array. Vistapro looks at such an elevation map and stretches each point on the grid up to its specified elevation, then textures the surfaces that lie between the points. Keep this basic premise in mind when experimenting with Vistapro, and you will begin to understand how very simple our world really is!

Basic Requirements

Vistapro is a sophisticated software program that uses the latest computer technology. To run Vistapro, you must have the following:

- IBM or compatible computer with 386 or better processor
- 4M RAM (at least 2M free XMS memory)
- Hard disk with at least 1M free
- VGA Graphics (or SVGA with VESA driver)
- DOS 3.0 or higher
- Microsoft-compatible mouse and driver

What Is Vistapro?

To quote from the Vistapro manual, "Vistapro is a three-dimensional landscape simulation program." Using the techniques described in Chapter 8 and data from Digital Elevation Model files, fractal landscapes are generated. Because Vistapro employs fractal landscape generation technology, it can also take any two-dimensional array and make a landscape from it. This includes everything from randomly generated fractals to any bitmap supplied by the user. That's right! It can even make a fractal landscape from a picture of your face.

The built-in fractal number generator enables you to create more than 4 billion terrain maps. With the PCX import facility, fractalizing, scaling, multiplying, and smoothing, the possibilities are endless. Some of the capabilities are not available in this demonstration version, however. To order a fully working copy of Vistapro, call the telephone number listed in Appendix A and on the Vistapro startup screen.

What You Can Do with Vistapro

Vistapro takes natural landscape or generated data, combines it with a user-defined camera and target position, and "snaps" a picture. It generates one picture at a time. You can specify an animation path, and sequential frames will be generated which you can play back as a 3-D movie. Using special controls, you can control various elements of your environment, such as sea level, trees, clouds, and rivers.

You have complete control of the colors Vistapro uses to paint the various portions of your image. You can save and restore these color palettes, so it is possible to have several at your disposal. You can rescale, smooth, or texturize your image. Special rendering controls include dithering and 24-bit image generation. For special 3-D effects, you can generate stereo pairs, anaglyphs, and three-view fly-throughs.

Where Vistapro Gets Its Data

The data Vistapro uses comes from the USGS Digital Elevation Maps. These files contain coordinate and elevation data at 30-meter increments. The USGS currently has approximately 40 percent of the contiguous United States mapped in this manner. Primarily, it covers national parks and areas around military bases. Vistapro handles four different sizes of DEM files. This demonstration version of the software has a tiny map embedded internally. It is of the El Capitan region of Yosemite National Park. You cannot load DEM files or save anything with this demo version.

What Is Vistapro Used For?

There are many uses for Vistapro. The most important use is fun. Vistapro is probably one of the most fun programs you will ever fiddle around with for under $150. There are practical applications as well. Scientists, engineers, artists, writers, teachers, game developers, and travelers will appreciate the hours of learning and fun they can have with Vistapro. Curious students of mathematics can spend hours exploring the worlds of the fractal generations and predetermined bitmap files.

III 3-D COMPUTER APPLICATIONS

Getting the Most Out of Vistapro

To get the most out of Vistapro, follow these simple tips:

- Do all your pre-renderings without clouds and trees and use polygon setting 8.
- Have *lots* of memory available.
- Leave Texture turned off until final renderings.
- Get a faster computer!

It is important to note that although Vistapro will take advantage of a floating-point processor, the base math is done in integer, so no appreciable speed increase can be obtained by using one.

Enough background. Let's make a landscape!

Getting Started—Your First Fractal Landscape

Run Vistapro by changing into the directory where it was installed (see the back of the book for installation instructions), typing **VISTA**, and pressing the Enter key. For example:

```
CD \QUE3D\VP
VISTA
```

When you see the credits screen, click the OK button at the top to clear it.

Now your screen should look like figure 10.1. At the top, you see a row of seven buttons that are the Vistapro menus. Directly below the menus is the topographic map of our landscape. This topographic map shows the X and Y, which are the coordinate axes for N, S, E, and W directions like a normal map. The elevation is indicated by color. Lowest elevations are blue to indicate sea level, lakes, or rivers, and the highest elevations are white to indicate snow cover. In-between areas are green, gray, and brown, as you might expect land masses and rocks to be.

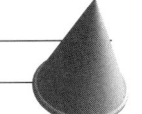

HANDS-ON WITH VISTAPRO

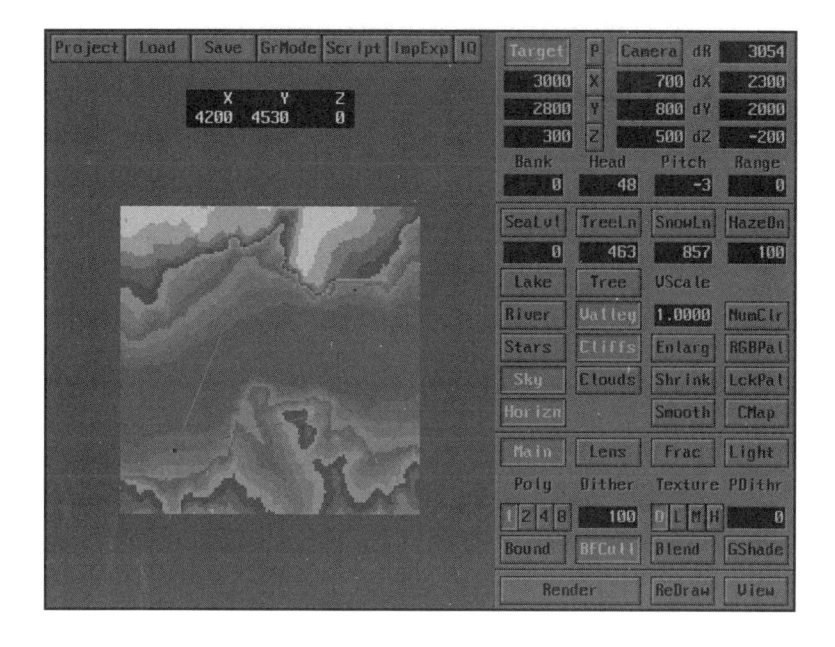

Figure 10.1

The Vistapro start-up screen.

On the right side of the screen is a multitude of buttons which control the Vistapro environment. We will investigate all of these buttons eventually, but for now click the IQ menu at the top of the screen and select Medium. This is the medium IQ script, which uses the system defaults for medium-quality rendering, plus adds two-dimensional trees and non-textured clouds. These settings will not provide the highest quality renderings, but are adequate for a first look. Further, the rendering time is moderate. Click the button at the bottom of the right side of the screen, labeled *Render*. Wait for a few moments, and your screen should look like figure 10.2.

Click the mouse to return to the control screen (or press the Esc key). Take a look at the screen and see exactly what you did. In the center of the screen on the right side, you see that six of the options buttons are highlighted. These are Sky, Horizn, Valley, Cliffs, Trees, and Clouds. These provide the basics for what you see on-screen. If you have a Super VGA and VESA driver, Vistapro rendered the image in 640×480×256 color mode. If not, it was done in 320×200×256 color mode, or standard low-resolution VGA. You can select the resolution by clicking the GrMode button at the top of the screen, and while holding down the mouse button, dragging down to the desired resolution. If you try to select a resolution that your hardware does not support, you will see a message indicating this fact.

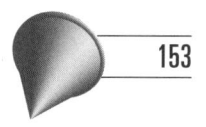

III 3-D COMPUTER APPLICATIONS

Figure 10.2

Your first fractal landscape.

Near the bottom of the screen on the right is a row of small buttons labeled *1*, *2*, *4*, and *8*. These indicate the polygon resolution of the drawing. A lower number (such as 1) means finer polygons and therefore, a more detailed image. To see how this works, click the *8* button, then click Render.

The image generated is much rougher than before. For the most part, a setting of 1 is sufficient for development work; however, if you want to work even more quickly while setting colors and objects, use 2, 4, or 8. To see a really incredible image, select Ultra from the IQ menu, then click Render again. Ultra sets all rendering options to their maximum settings for the highest quality output. This image takes quite a while to render, but it is a shortcut to some of the advanced options we will discuss later. If you don't want to wait for the Ultra rendering, press the Esc key to abort the rendering and go on to the next section (it takes approximately 15 minutes on a 486/25). If you want to view the last image you rendered, click the View button in the bottom right corner of the screen.

Back to Basics—The Vistapro Menus

Vistapro is controlled through a series of menus. These menus enable you to set up the program, load and save data, and save animation sequences. The following paragraphs look at each menu individually.

The Project Menu

Vistapro has seven menus at the top of the screen. In this demonstration version, many of the options have been disabled. In the Project menu, everything is enabled except for Set DEM Size and Spawn DOS. The other functions enable you to see the setting currently in use by Vistapro and to quit the program.

The Load and Save Menus

The Load and Save menus are totally disabled in this version. In the complete version, they enable you to load DEM files, backgrounds, and PCX files, and to save all your work, settings, and results.

The GrMode Menu

All of the options in GrMode are enabled in this version, except that you are limited to 640×480×256 as the highest resolution. Enable 24 bit tells Vistapro to save a 24-bit image in memory, which is useless because you can't save it anyway, so don't bother turning it on. It is useful if you want to play with the RGBPal button later.

The Script and ImpExp Menus

Script files and ImpExp are disabled in the demonstration version of Vistapro. Scripts enable you to make animation paths and generate fly-throughs. There is also an external utility that allows you to make curved, realistic paths. ImpExp enables you to convert between various file formats.

III 3-D COMPUTER APPLICATIONS

The IQ Menu

The IQ menu enables you to select an IQ script. This is a special script file that is user-configurable. The IQ menu is enabled in the demo version of Vistapro, but you cannot use the User IQ script. The other IQ scripts are shortcuts to various settings so that you can generate quick renderings without fiddling with all the buttons. You can simply run Vistapro, select a camera and a target position, and run an IQ script, which generates the quality rendering you want.

In the full commercial version of Vistapro, the User IQ script is useful for working on extensive projects such as animations, where several days of renderings need to take place to complete the sequence and the program must be stopped and restarted several times. It would be a lot of extra work to have to set up all the buttons each time you started the program. User IQ scripts make this unnecessary.

The next sections take you through a succession of operations to generate a very high-quality image. To save time, each section begins with a summary box that tells you how to set up everything done so far. Because you cannot save scripts or sessions in this version of the software, this is the only way to remain consistent. By running the software and doing everything in the summary box, your program and the illustrations in the book will stay in sync. If this is not important to you, you can skip the summary boxes.

Tutorial 1—Selecting a View

The most basic form of control over Vistapro is telling the program where you want to stand and what you want to look at. You do this by setting the camera and target locations (see fig. 10.3).

Setting Your Target

The left column in the top right of the screen is labeled *Target*. There are ways to set the Target, or the point at which your camera is pointed. Remember that we are in real-world, three-dimensional coordinates. The target position has three coordinates associated with it: the X and Y location as seen on the topographic map in the main area of the screen, and the Z coordinate (elevation).

HANDS-ON WITH VISTAPRO

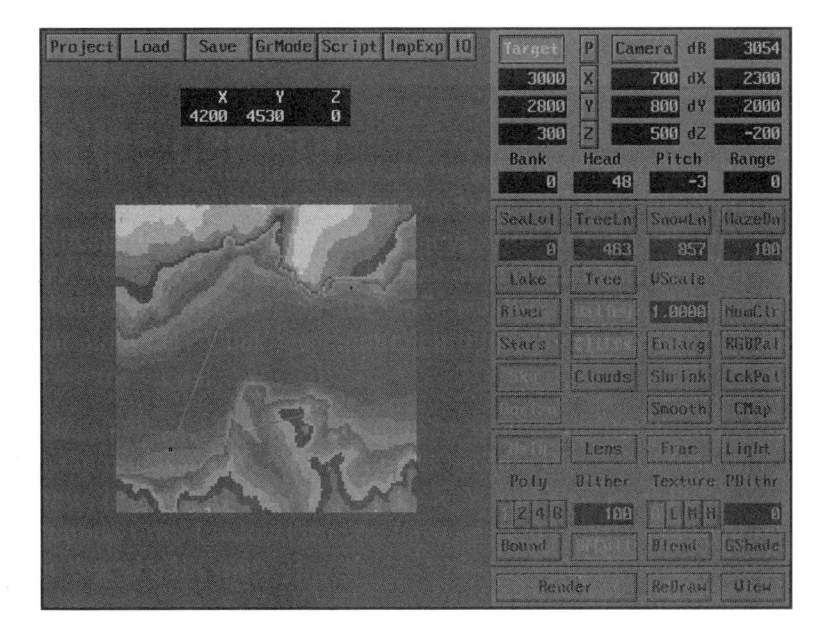

Figure 10.3

The Vistapro Target and Camera settings.

To set the target location, press the Target button and click the topographic map in the location you want. The elevation is automatically set to the elevation at that location. If you click a blue area, the target will be set to the elevation of that lake, river, or sea. If you click a white region, the target will be set to the elevation of that mountain. Click several different target locations and re-render to see the views.

You can also set the target location by typing coordinates directly. Vistapro uses meters for coordinates because that is how the data comes from the USGS. Click in the X, Y, and Z areas and type numbers until the location you have selected looks about right on the topographic map.

Setting the Camera

The camera position is set in much the same way as the target. Remember that Camera is where you are and Target is where you are looking. On the topographic map, the camera is indicated by a little black circle with two lines radiating from it. These lines show the camera's field of view. Later, you will see how to adjust this field of view.

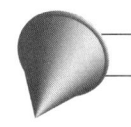

III 3-D COMPUTER APPLICATIONS

To set the camera position, click the Camera button at the top of the screen. Like the target, the camera position is set by simply clicking in the topographic map at the location you want. Notice how the field of view lines always change to point toward the target. This is a good indicator of what your view will look like.

There is one major difference between how the target and camera are set when you create them by clicking on the topographic map. To avoid any possible confusion relating to having your camera underground or even exactly at ground level, the default is to have the camera placed 100 meters above the current elevation. Of course, you can always move your camera to ground level or below; but to be safe, always keep it about 50 to 100 meters above the ground. This avoids problems such as being under water or being directly behind a tree.

Both the camera and target settings share the X, Y, and Z buttons. To tell which is currently active, look at the Target and Camera buttons and see which is selected. To the right of Target and Camera is a row of buttons labeled *dR*, *dX*, *dY*, and *dZ*. These are the distances along the direct path (dR), the X-axis (dX), Y-axis (dY), and elevation or Z-axis (dZ). If you set your camera and target and just want to change the direct distance, adjust the dR value. The target remains fixed and the camera is moved to the proper distance. This functionality is useful when setting key frames for an animation sequence.

Click on several target and camera positions and render the frames to get a feel for how to use the system. Pay particular attention to the dZ variable. If it is negative, you are looking down. If it is positive, you are looking up. Sometimes it is interesting to look straight down on a region. Enter the following coordinates:

	Target	Camera
X	2500	2500
Y	2700	2700
Z	800	1500

This results in a straight-down view of El Capitan. Later, after you purchase the complete version of Vistapro, generate a stereo pair and anaglyph of this view. It will look like figure 10.4, but in 3-D!

The *P* button for Perspective Viewing

Sometimes you need a shortcut to change the view you are currently looking at. The view is close to what you want, but you want little changes. This is where the magic *P* button comes in. Start by resetting the program defaults by rerunning the program or entering the following coordinates for Camera and Target:

	Target	Camera
X	3000	700
Y	2800	800
Z	300	500

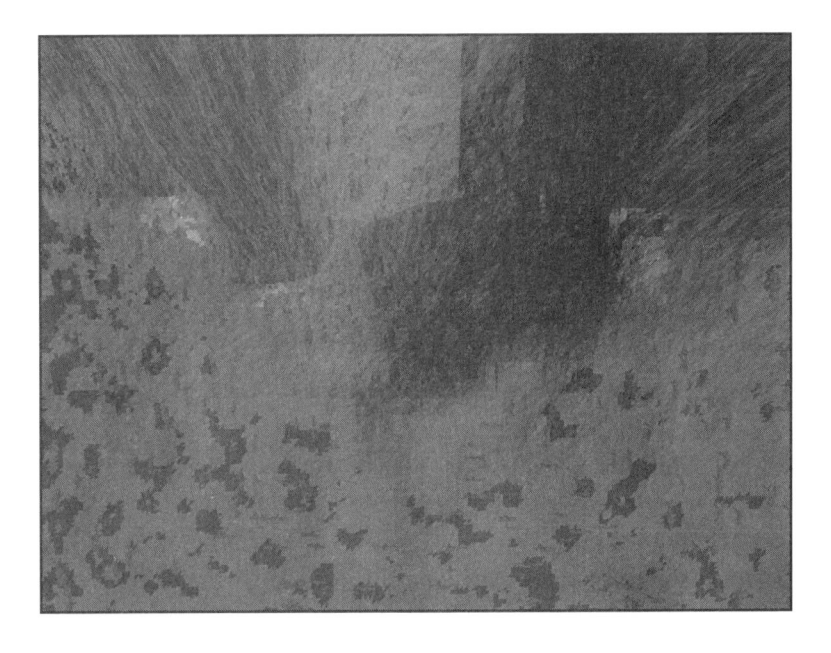

Figure 10.4

A bird's-eye view of El Capitan in stereo.

After you have set these coordinates, click the *P* button between Camera and Target. The *P* button generates a perspective view in the topographic map area. Your screen should look like figure 10.5.

By clicking in this view, you can adjust the target position, and thus, your view. Click in several locations until you have a view you like. To zoom in or out, press the up-arrow and down-arrow keys.

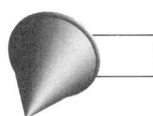

III 3-D COMPUTER APPLICATIONS

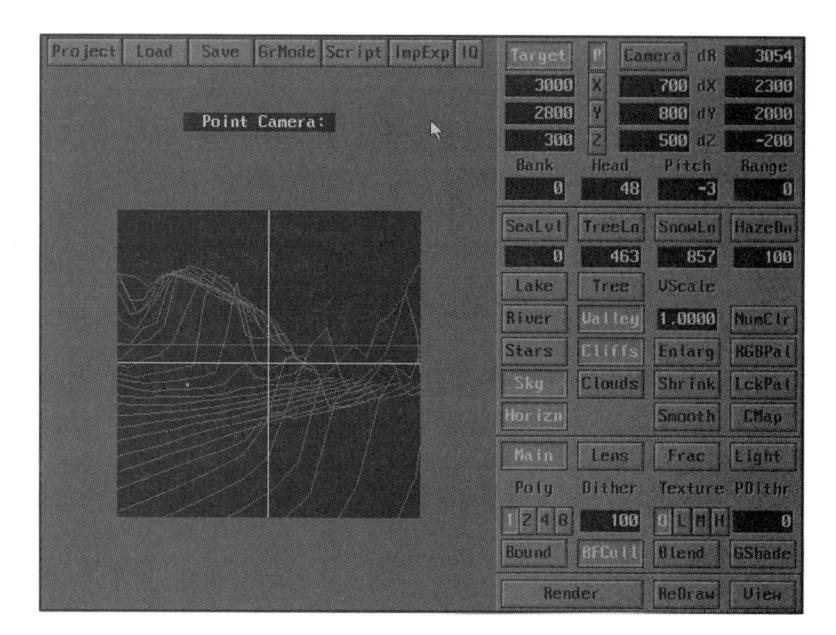

Figure 10.5

Perspective view.

When you have settled on a view you are happy with, click with the right mouse button to return to the topographic view. Notice how the Target position has changed but the Camera has not. Experiment with this function until you are comfortable with its operation.

Bank, Head, Pitch, and Range

So far, you've seen how to place yourself and look at something. But that isn't all there is to a realistic view. The following paragraphs tell you how to look up, look down, and tilt the camera for more interesting views.

Bank

To set the angle of the camera along its own longitudinal or Y axis, adjust the Bank setting. A positive value causes clockwise rotation. A negative value causes counter-clockwise rotation. This effect is necessary for realistic fly-throughs in which the motion of an airplane is to be simulated. The effect of rotation of the camera is to have the picture that is generated appear to rotate in the opposite direction. Bank here means the same as a banked turn on a racetrack. If you are turning to the right, you want a clockwise or positive bank value.

Head

Head values tell at which angle the camera is pointed according to its own Z or vertical axis. This is the same as rotating your head left or right. Bank takes precedence over Head, so if the camera is already banked, the head setting is relative to the camera's new position. This is like laying on your side, then rotating your head left and right. Relative to you, the movement is left and right; however, relative to the ground, it is now up and down.

Pitch

Pitch is rotation about the camera's X axis. This setting adjusts whether the camera is looking up (like looking up toward your forehead) or down (like looking toward your chin). As in the Head settings, this motion is relative to the camera, not the universe. It has nothing to do with the mountains or trees you have created.

Range

The range button tells Vistapro not to render anything farther away than the set value. For example, if you set it to 1000, objects farther away than 1000 meters will not be rendered, thus rendering time is faster. This is most useful when you are rendering test animations. If the important things are close to you, you can render a sequence faster without wasting time on faraway objects. If you want to test to see whether you are flying through trees, this is a good button to use.

Play around with the Bank, Head, and Pitch settings to generate some interesting views. When you are through, take a break and quit the program to get ready for the next section. In it, we explore the rest of the Vistapro world.

III 3-D COMPUTER APPLICATIONS

Tutorial 2—Adding Objects to Your Vistapro World

Now that you can control your position and view, things get interesting. In this section, you learn how to put various atmospheric and environmental effects into operation.

Sea Level, Tree Line, Snow Line, and Haze Density

Sea Level

Sea level indicates the elevation at which rendering starts. By setting the sea level to a positive value, your entire landscape sinks into the sea. The sea level value gets reset for 0, and the other elevations are reduced by the amount you entered for sea level. For example, if you enter a value of 1000 for sea level, 5000-meter mountains become 4000 meters. Sea level is always 0. To see this effect, click the SeaLvl button and click the dark green region of the landscape in the topographic view. You should get a sea level value of about 100 to 110. Vistapro asks if you want to erase old rivers and lakes. Answer yes for now. It also asks if you want to generate waves. Say yes so that you can see how they look. You are then asked if the sea is acceptable—answer *yes*.

> This is the beginning, so to reset, just start the program from scratch!

At this point, your screen should look like figure 10.6. The waves on the water are very rough, but you can smooth those out later when you get to the rendering controls. To make this tutorial concise, set the sea level to 100, answer yes to the delete rivers and lakes question, and accept the waves and sea level as before. Everything at elevations of up to 100 meters is now underwater, so it is colored blue. It doesn't really look like a sea, but that doesn't matter for now.

Tree Line

The tree line is automatically set to 1/3 of the height of the tallest mountain in your landscape. There are four kinds of trees in Vistapro. The different trees are divided equally through that region from sea level to the tree line. In other words, tree type 1 is drawn in the first quarter of the tree region, tree 2 in the second, and so on. This is useful if you want to have palm trees at sea level and pine trees at the higher elevations. More on this later under the discussion of the Tree button. For now, leave the TreeLn button alone, but be aware that it sets the upper elevation at which trees are drawn. This is the same as the timber line in mountain regions.

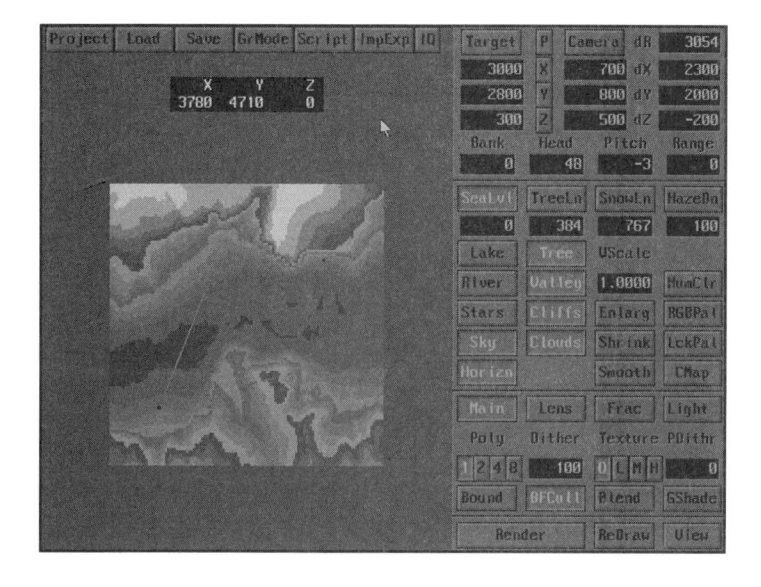

Figure 10.6

Sea-level setting at 100.

Snow Line

Snow line is exactly like tree line except that it is automatically set to approximately 2/3 of the highest elevation. Everything above this elevation is rendered in white to indicate snow. To remove snow altogether, set the snow line very high. To generate a Winter scene, set the snow line to a low level. Almost the entire scene will be white. For now, leave this value alone as well.

Haze Density

The HazeDn button tells Vistapro at what density to generate haze. Haze is a parameter that is used to generate realistic horizons. If you have ever looked out across a horizon, you have noticed that things are hazy when they are far away. This is a natural atmospheric condition that can be simulated with the HazeDn button. Note that this is *not* fog. Fog has a lower elevation and an upper elevation. It is a special type of cloud. Haze is an atmospheric condition. However, the proper setting of HazeDn can appear to be fog under the proper conditions.

The most important function of HazeDn is to make the sky color fade at the horizon. If HazeDn is set to 0, the sky is one color all the way to the ground, which is very unrealistic. A higher number for HazeDn means more haze, and 0 means none. If you set it to 0, your image will be very crisp and clear, but will not look very realistic. For our tutorial purposes, the default setting of 100 will suffice.

Sky, Horizn, Valley, and Cliffs

Sky and Horizn are not configurable options, but allow you to turn off and on the horizon and sky. To see how they work, toggle them off by clicking both buttons and then the Render button. The sky will be black. In the current scene, the horizon line is completely covered, but you probably noticed that the mountains started rendering on a totally black screen rather than the usual blue sky and green landmass.

1. Run Vistapro.
2. Set SeaLvl to 100, and answer *yes* to the "Erase old Rivers/Lakes/Seas?" dialog box. Answer yes to the "Accept sea?" and "Generate waves?" dialog boxes.

The Valley button allows you to set the distance up the walls of the valleys that trees can grow beyond the normal tree line and also how far below the snow line the snow can come. Click the Valley button to turn it off, then click it again to turn it on. You will see the dialog box in figure 10.7.

There are two options in this dialog box, Valley width and Magnitude. Valley width tells the number of units around each elevation point that the valley function will operate, and Magnitude is a scaling factor. The defaults are 8 and 100 respectively, which means that the valley function will be calculated at each point by looking at the points up to 8 units away, and the default Magnitude is 100 percent. A Magnitude of 0 turns off the valley function. For now, leave it set to the defaults by clicking OK.

The Cliffs button enables you to set the minimum slope that is to be considered a cliff by Vistapro. This is important because it causes the cliff regions specified to be colored with the gray colors of the palette and to not have much in the way of trees and snow. Click the Cliffs button to turn it off, then click again to turn it on. You will see a dialog box (see fig. 10.8) that asks you to input the slope value (cliff threshold). The default value is 30. This means that cliffs of slope greater than 30 will not hold snow or grow trees. This is a realistic number for natural land masses. Leave it at the default for now.

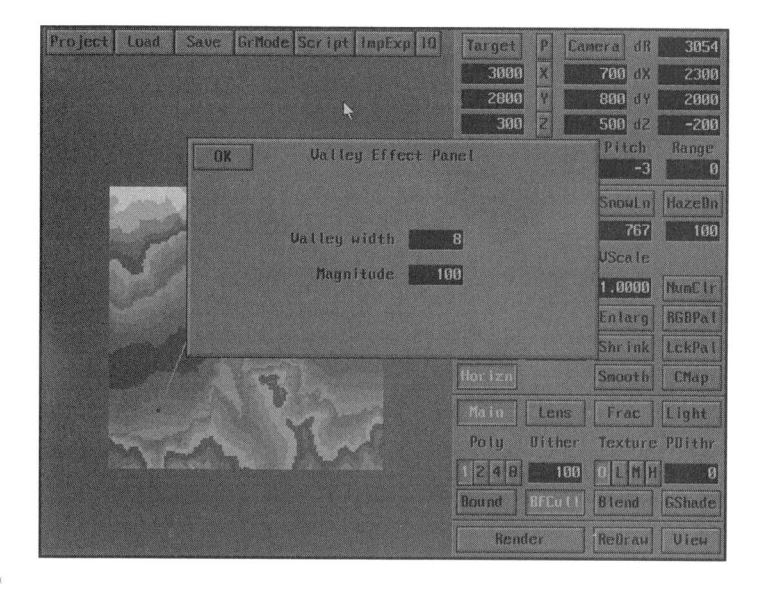

Figure 10.7

The Valley Effect Panel.

Lakes and Rivers

Lakes and rivers are interesting objects. With these features, you can create bodies of water where there are none in the real world. This is the beginning of the omnipotent feeling you get when playing around with Vistapro. In a way, you *are* omnipotent. You are creating a world of your very own!

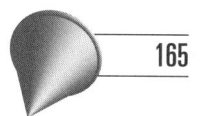

III 3-D COMPUTER APPLICATIONS

The Lake button enables you to select an elevation from the topographic map, then choose whether you want all areas of the map that lie below that elevation to be underwater. To experiment with lakes, click the Lake button, then point to an area of the topographic map where you want a lake to be. If you look at the X, Y, and Z coordinates directly above the topographic map, you will see the elevation at that point is the Z coordinate. Click the mouse button, and you will get a dialog box that asks you to set the desired lake level (see fig. 10.9). The default is the height where you clicked. Click OK, and you will see a dark green grid overlaid on your image, which is a graphic indication of what your lake will look like if you accept it. If you say *yes*, Vistapro starts at the lowest elevation in the valley and fills with water everything up to the elevation you specified in the Lake dialog. For now, answer *no* to the Accept lake? question. For this tutorial, we don't want any lakes, but we will make a river.

1. Run Vistapro.

2. Set SeaLvl to 100, and answer *yes* to the "Erase old Rivers/Lakes/Seas?" dialog box. Answer *yes* to the "Accept sea?" and "Generate waves?" dialog boxes.

3. Make sure Sky, Horizn, Valley, and Cliffs are turned on.

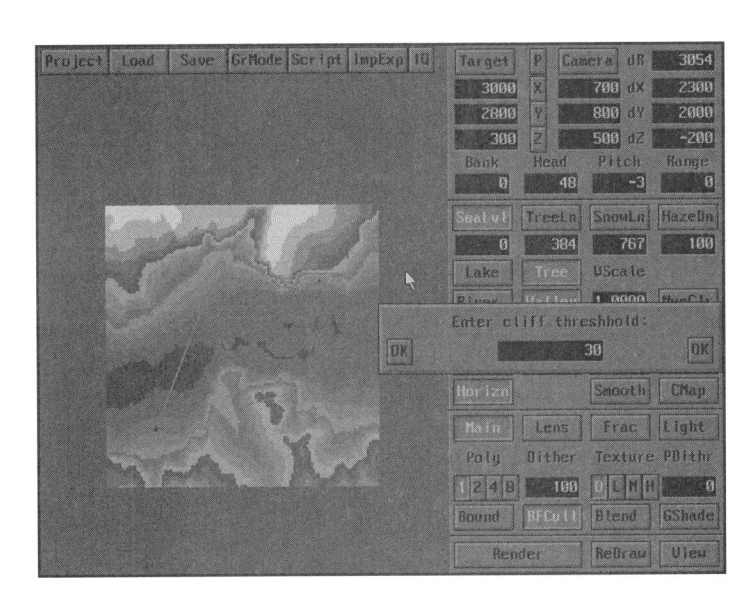

Figure 10.8

The Enter cliff threshold dialog box.

166

HANDS-ON WITH VISTAPRO

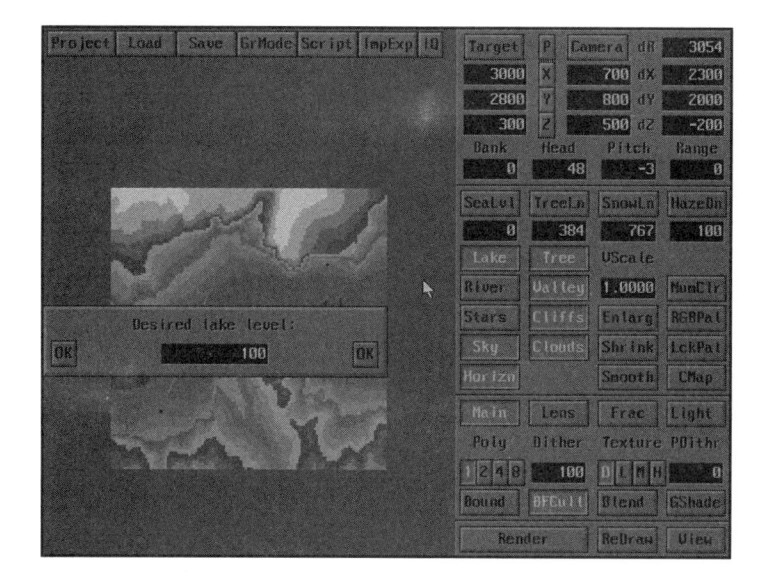

Figure 10.9

The Desired lake level dialog box.

River works similarly to Lake, except that instead of filling up from the bottom, the water tends to seek its way downhill. If the level of the ground is lower, it fills the surrounding area until it reaches the starting elevation and overflows, then continues downhill. A river will continue to be created until it reaches another water mass or the edge of the map.

To see how it works, click the River button, then move the mouse cursor until you are at approximately X=2220, Y=120 and click again. A green grid will again be placed over the projected river (much like the Lake function), and you are asked whether you want to accept the river. Because the last place you clicked was the river source, the dialog box appears at this location and covers up your river, so it is difficult to see. Just click anywhere else on the screen to move the dialog box out of the way. This time, answer *yes* to accept the river. Click the Render button to see your masterpiece. You will see that you have not only created a river, but a waterfall! Not bad for your first day as world builder. (This is actually Bridal Veil falls in Yosemite.)

167

III 3-D COMPUTER APPLICATIONS

Stars

The Stars button simply tells Vistapro to generate a starfield if you want to have a night scene. If you click the Stars button, you get a dialog box asking whether you want double-height and double-width stars. This gives you some control over the appearance of your stars. If you select stars while you have Sky turned on, the haze portion of the sky will still be rendered, giving a twilight sort of look. If you turn it off, your scene looks like the dead of night. Try this: Click the Stars button and answer no to both questions. Then click the Render button. Notice the haze level reaching partway up into the sky.

1. Run Vistapro.
2. Set SeaLvl to 100, and answer *yes* to the "Erase old Rivers/Lakes/Seas?" dialog box. Answer *yes* to the "Accept sea?" and "Generate waves?" dialog boxes.
3. Make sure Sky, Horizn, Valley, and Cliffs are turned on.
4. Click on River, then click near location 2220,120 on the topographic map and accept the river.

Now click the Sky button to turn it off, and press Render again. This time, you get solid black sky all the way down to the horizon. This can be useful when dealing with abstract renderings, but for normal moonlit, natural scenes, stick to leaving the Sky button on. Turn Sky back on and turn Stars off by clicking their respective buttons.

Note: In the full version of Vistapro, you can use the Background function in the Load menu to use any bitmap of your choice for the background rather than the computer-generated sky.

Tree

To understand the Tree button, you must explore its control panel box. The Tree function is turned off in the demo version of Vistapro, but we will explore it anyway. You can generate trees by using the Med, High, and Ultra IQ scripts. For purposes of demonstration, load the Med IQ Script, then click on Tree to enter the Tree Control Panel (see fig. 10.10).

HANDS-ON WITH VISTAPRO

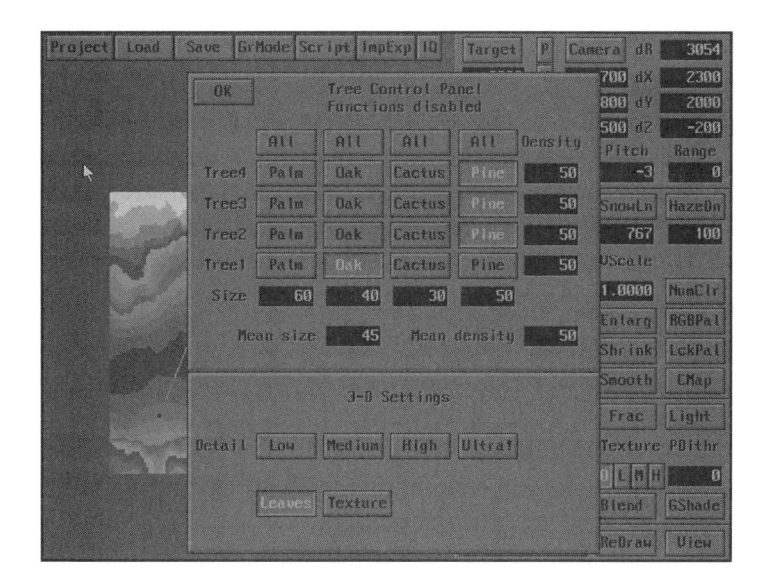

Figure 10.10

The Tree Control Panel with IQ Script MED.

As stated earlier, there are four different types of trees available in Vistapro. They are Palm, Oak, Cactus, and Pine. There are also four different levels at which trees can exist. These are levels Tree1 through Tree4. Each type of tree can have an average size associated with it. Each level of tree can have a different density associated with it. The four levels of trees are divided evenly up to the Tree Line. This means that if the Tree Line is set to 400, Tree1 will exist up to 100 meters, Tree2 will exist up to 200 meters, and so on.

You can set any combination of trees at any level. In fact, you can have all types of trees at all levels, which gives the appearance of a jungle. In this script, the trees are set with Tree1 as Oak and Tree2, Tree3, and Tree4 all as Pine. Note the default sizes and densities. Each level can have its own average size and density of tree cover. These parameters are set to provide interesting results with this sample landscape.

1. Run Vistapro.

2. Set SeaLvl to 100, and answer *yes* to the "Erase old Rivers/Lakes/Seas?" dialog box. Answer *yes* to the "Accept sea?" and "Generate waves?" dialog boxes.

3. Make sure Sky, Horizn, Valley, and Cliffs are turned on.

4. Click on River, then click near location 2220,120 on the topographic map and accept the river.

169

III 3-D COMPUTER APPLICATIONS

At the bottom of the control panel are the 3-D detail settings. These enable you to set 3-D tree generation on, set the detail level from Low to Ultra, and to set the Leaves and Texture on or off. With the detail set high and the leaves and texture turned on, rendering will be slow, but the results are incredible. Leaves should be left off if you are rendering fall or winter scenes. The Texture button applies fractal texture to the leaves, branches, and bark of your image. Unless you are going to have close-ups of your trees, this function serves no purpose. For this script, we are sticking to 2-D trees, so these settings have no effect. To see fancier trees, select Ultra from the IQ Scripts menu.

For future renderings in the tutorial, we will leave these settings alone, but we will turn off the Tree button to speed up renderings while exploring other features.

Click OK to accept these settings, then click Render and get a cup of coffee. Be quick, though! Even though we are generating water, clouds, and trees, it takes only approximately 1 minute to render this scene on a 486/25.

The image you just generated should look almost exactly like the first image you generated, except for the presence of the water you created with SeaLvl and Rivers. All along, there have been clouds in the sky as a result of the IQ Script. Let's look into clouds and see how they are generated in Vistapro.

Clouds

Vistapro generates clouds by using fractals in much the same way it generates landscapes. The Cloud Control Panel is turned off in the demo version, but we will look at it anyway to learn how it works. The IQ scripts select increasingly complex cloud masses. Click the Clouds button. You will see the Cloud Control Panel (see fig. 10.11).

The first button in the Cloud Control Panel is the Fractal Detail button. This acts similarly to the Texture button in Trees. If it is on, fractal details and thus more realism will result in your clouds. Of course, this will slow down rendering, but not by much.

The Density setting tells Vistapro how thick the cloud mass should be. The maximum value here is 100. A medium value is most realistic, so it is set at 50. The Hardness setting tells Vistapro how fluffy to make the clouds. For fluffier clouds, use a lower number. Higher numbers result in hard-edged clouds, like very high cirrus clouds.

Altitude indicates the mean altitude of the cloud mass. The only time you really need to set this is if you want to raise the camera higher. Vistapro will not allow you to put the camera higher than the clouds, so if you try, it automatically moves the clouds higher.

> 1. Run Vistapro.
> 2. Set SeaLvl to 100, and answer *yes* to the "Erase old Rivers/Lakes/Seas?" dialog box. Answer *yes* to the "Accept sea?" and "Generate waves?" dialog boxes.
> 3. Make sure Sky, Horizn, Valley, and Cliffs are turned on.
> 4. Click on River, then click near location 2220,120 on the topographic map and accept the river.
> 5. Select IQ Script MED from the IQ menu.

Farther down the page are four buttons labeled *S*, *M*, *L*, and *X*. These are indicators of the cloud size. The *S* button yields lots of small clouds, and *X* yields a few large cloud masses. Once you have changed this setting, you need to click the Generate Clouds button to generate a new cloud mass. Even if you don't want to change the size of the clouds, but want a different pattern, you can generate a new pattern by clicking the Generate Clouds button.

In the demo version of Vistapro, a different cloud mass is generated every time you start the program. The full version of the software enables you to save your cloud mass so that it is always the same. This is important if you are working on a project and want to preserve the same look throughout.

The last button is one of the most interesting. It takes the current DEM file and generates a cloud mass from it. This has several possibilities. For now, you can load any file you want as a PCX file, make a DEM from it, and project it into a cloud mass. This works for effects like sky-writing. Also, if you take the current landscape and project it into the sky, you get a mirror image of the land as clouds. Although this isn't always obvious from looking at the results, it is a neat special effect.

III 3-D COMPUTER APPLICATIONS

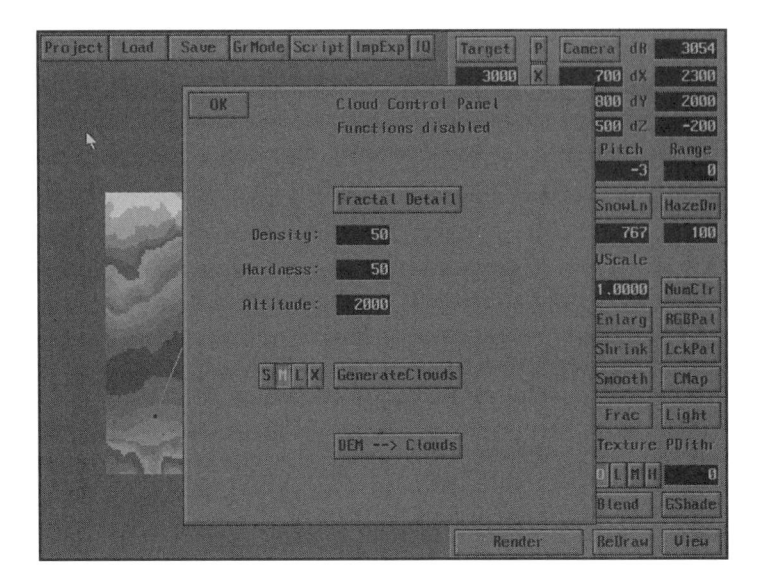

Figure 10.11

The Cloud Control Panel.

The rendering you did in the Tree section is the same as you would get now, so don't bother rendering at this time. Later, load a higher IQ Script (High or Ultra) and see if you can tell the difference in the quality of the clouds. Both allow fractal detail, which adds a great deal of texture and realism.

VScale, Enlarg, Shrink, and Smooth

The next column of options on the middle of the control panel enables you to vertically scale your entire model, zoom into it, pull back from it, or smooth it out. This offers you a complete set of tools for manipulating your landscape. By zooming in and increasing the texture, you can get more realistic close-ups of virtually any region.

VScale is handy if you want to make DEM files that are not physically similar to each other. For example, if you want to gradually change from a map of Yosemite to a map of your face, the average highs and lows should be similar to provide a smooth effect. VScale affects only the vertical components, so it also has the effect of making vertical surfaces look more dramatic. You can make cliffs steeper and valleys deeper.

Enlarge and Shrink take any region of the DEM file and enlarge and shrink it. This sounds simple, but remember that even 30-meter increments aren't very finite. A lot can happen in 100 feet of landscape. By taking a region and enlarging it, then re-fractalizing it (an option under the Fractal button that we will cover later), you can add detail that previously wasn't there.

The Enlarge button enables you to select either interpolation or duplication for generating the in-between points after scaling. The difference is that duplication generates a jagged surface because it just uses existing points (a steep hill becomes stair-stepped) and interpolation retains a smooth surface because it averages the surrounding points. The Shrink button will reduce a landscape down as far as 66×66 points. It is mostly used for reducing rendering times when detail is not important. Smaller landscapes render faster because there is less work to do.

Smoothing a landscape has the effect of removing protruding edges and jaggedness. This is used most often when fixing up fractal landscapes. The realistic DEM files are accurate data and do not need to be smoothed. However, sometimes a snow-covered peak will not hold snow properly if it is too jagged. Remember from the discussion on Cliffs that certain slopes will not hold snow. If you want a peak to hold snow more evenly, smoothing it provides some assistance. By smoothing it, you can remove some of the greater-than-threshold slopes.

NumClr, RGBPal, LckPal, and CMap

The NumClr parameter enables you to set the number of colors you want Vistapro to reduce the rendered image to in 256-color modes. Sometimes it is useful to restrict this number, because you might be integrating the images or sequence into an existing Multimedia shell program or other application.

To change the number of colors, click the NumClr button and enter the number of colors you want, then click OK. Vistapro starts at color 0 and uses as many colors as you specify, leaving the top of the palette clear.

RGBPal tells Vistapro to take the current 24-bit image in memory (you must have Enable 24-bit turned on in the GrMode menu) and generate a palette from it. This is most useful when you are generating a single image and want the best colors used. For example, if you are close to the water and would like more blues than normally generated, you would render a 24-bit image, select RGBPal, then re-render to that palette. Normally, the palette is somewhat fixed; however, this control enables you to improve rendering quality.

LckPal allows you to lock the current color palette so that Vistapro won't go through the palette-making process every time you render. This has two very important uses. First, it speeds rendering time during development. Normally, Vistapro makes a new palette every time you move the camera. With the palette locked, it just uses the last palette generated. The other more important use is for generating animation sequences. Many animation formats do not support palette changes on a frame-by-frame basis. By generating a palette in advance and locking it, you can render an entire sequence to the same palette, which makes for smoother animation.

CMap is the Vistapro color map. This is not a palette setting box. Actual palettes are generated at render time. CMap is a set of controls which tell Vistapro which colors to use to paint different portions of the image. Click the CMap button and you get a full-screen ColorMap Control Panel. Each of the objects identified in the Control Panel (see fig. 10.12) has its own color assigned to it. This is the base color to paint with. Vistapro alters it slightly during rendering to compensate for haze, shadows, and general lighting.

To change any particular color, click its button. You will see the color for that button, as well as several surrounding buttons. To adjust its color, slide the RGB or HSV sliders up and down until the color you want is obtained. Clicking on any other button locks that color into place.

In true-color rendering, each color from the color map can generate hundreds of shades in the final rendering. The defaults are set to resemble a springtime color set. If you want to create a surrealistic sunset, you might set the sky colors to orange and red. To generate springtime, change the tree colors to bright purples and pinks to look like blossoms.

HANDS-ON WITH VISTAPRO

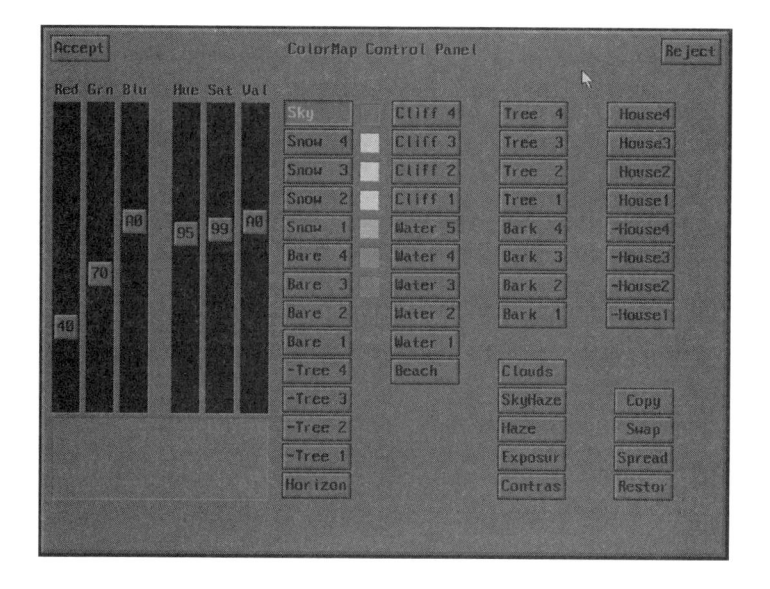

Figure 10.12

The ColorMap Control Panel.

On the lower right of the Control Panel are settings for haze, exposure, contrast, and other environmental factors. These are very useful for generating special effects. For example, if you set the Haze and SkyHaze to 0, then go back and set the HazeDn to a high number such as 400, a foggy nighttime scene is created. To remove all surrounding environment, set Sky and Ocean to black and set Haze to 0. This makes it look like your landscape is floating in surrealistic space. Millions of combinations are possible.

At the far right are buttons for copying and swapping colors, creating smooth gradients between colors, and restoring the original palette that was set when you entered the control panel. The use of these buttons is straightforward, with the exception of Swap. To swap any two colors, click on the first color, then click the Swap button, then click on the second color. The colors will transpose positions. The Spread button is useful for generating smooth transitions between similar parts of the landscape, such as bare ground. You might spread Bare 1 to Bare 4 using dark brown to tan. This gives the illusion of higher elevation being better lit. Although the result is not always realistic, many interesting combinations are there for you to uncover.

Experiment and have fun with the Color Map functionality. For now, to keep this tutorial aligned with the real world, reject the fiddling you may have done, and leave the defaults set.

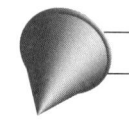

III 3-D COMPUTER APPLICATIONS

Improving the Rendering

We have covered controlling the view and controlling your environment. Now it is time to control the actual output image. These are the most-used buttons in the program and are found at the lower right panel on the main screen. This panel is actually four subpanels labeled Main, Lens, Frac, and Light. As you might expect, Main enables you to control the basic rendering parameters. Lens controls depth of view and special effects such as stereo images and three-monitor fly-throughs. Frac allows you to generate fractal landscapes, and Light enables you to control the lighting on the landscape. Let's look at them one at a time.

Main

In this section, you will re-render several times to see the effect of the controls, so set up the system as in the preceding Summary Box.

I spoke briefly about the Poly controls in the introduction to this chapter. Poly sets the polygon size that Vistapro generates in drawing the landscape. A setting of 1 sets small polygons, whereas a setting of 8 makes the largest. You have used 1 for most drawing because speed wasn't really important. For much of this section, you will want to render as fast as possible to check things, so click on the Poly button labeled 8. Click the Tree and Clouds buttons to turn them off, then click Render. The result appears in figure 10.13.

1. Run Vistapro.
2. Set SeaLvl to 100, answer *yes* to the "delete rivers and lakes" dialog box, and answer *yes* to the "generate waves?" dialog box.
3. Make sure Sky, Horizn, Valley, and Cliffs are turned on.
4. Click on River, click near location 2220,120 on the topographic map, and accept the river.
5. Select IQ Script MED from the IQ menu.

The landscape you just generated is very choppy and not very interesting. This is partly because of the 8 setting, but it's also partly because of the fact that this is a demo landscape that is very small, so large polygons really destroy it. By setting Poly to 2, you will see the quality and speed most likely to be expected for real landscapes and the full version of the software. I suggest 2 for this tutorial because it has enough quality to see things such as view and lighting.

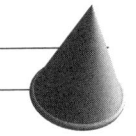

Dither is a number that tells Vistapro how much to overlap regions. You set Tree Line earlier; however, the landscape wouldn't be very interesting if all trees stopped exactly at the tree line. Also, the different types of trees overlap slightly in the real world, so this allows that realistic overlap. A setting of 100 is the default and is best for most applications, so leave it set there.

Figure 10.13

A landscape with Poly set to 8.

Texture is the fractal texturing applied to each polygon. Our MED IQ Script sets it to 0, which means no texture. This is fine for fast renderings. Each polygon is drawn as a flat polygon. But for realistic cliffs and rocks, more texture is needed. To see the difference, click on Render again to render the current image. Now click on M in the texture buttons. You see a dialog box asking whether you want altitude or shading textures. Altitude yields a more rough, natural rocky look, whereas shading yields a smoother look. Because you are generating rocks, click Altitude. Now click Render again. This takes a little longer to render than with Texture off. Can you see the difference?

Click on Texture 0 again so that future renderings won't be slowed down.

PDithr means *pixel dither*. This is dithering to artificially smooth out the image in 256-color modes. People with experience in image processing are familiar with this process. Click in the region under

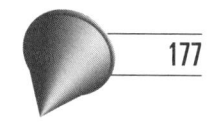

III 3-D COMPUTER APPLICATIONS

PDithr and enter a number of approximately 200. You see a dialog box asking you whether you want random or ordered dithering. Random is random error distribution and ordered is a pattern fill. Pattern fill is better for pre-renderings, so click on Ordered. Now click on Render again. Notice how the sky appears to smooth out. This feature has no effect on 24-bit images, so if you prefer to see dithering in your screen previews, turn it on. If not, leave it off. We will leave it set to 200 for the tutorial.

The Bound button enables you to set a region inside your landscape which marks the limits of Vistapro rendering. This can be very useful if you know that particular regions are not in the field of view. Although Vistapro does not generate polygons for regions outside the screen area, it must analyze them to make that determination. By using boundaries, you can eliminate that analysis, and thus save valuable time.

BFCull tells Vistapro not to bother rendering the back faces of objects. This is a standard 3-D program option that you should leave on at all times. Only in special cases will you want to set BFCull off. These include instances in which the camera is at such an angle that some of the back faces are visible.

The Blend button reduces the coarseness of the landscape at a distance. It has the effect of *anti-aliasing* or smoothing faraway regions. It also has the side effect of washing out the color slightly because it works by averaging the colors of the surrounding polygons, so use it with caution. For very high-end renderings, its use is recommended for added realism.

GShade is Gouroud shading. This is a special type of light shading that is used in 3-D modeling. It is very slow and tends to smooth out the landscape; however, in some cases you may find it useful. The biggest use is in rendering where you are very close to a tree or rock. It has the effect of smoothing the lighting on near polygons. A combination of altitude texture and Gouroud shading results in natural-looking surfaces.

Lens

The Lens controls enable you to set the field of view, generate stereo pairs, and make a three-monitor fly-through. The stereo pair generation and three-monitor options are controllable only through scripts and manipulation of files, so they aren't very useful in this demo version of the software. However, it's worth taking the time to learn how they work.

The top of the Lens panel has two buttons, Wide and Zoom, and an area to enter a custom number. This number is the focal length for the camera. A value of 16 yields a 90-degree field of view, whereas 32 yields a 45-degree field of view. These are the values that are entered if you click either the Wide or Zoom button, respectively. For other values, click in the region and enter a number of your choice. For most landscapes, a Zoom value of 16 is a good number, and it is the default.

Port and Strbrd tell Vistapro to turn the camera to its left and right, respectively. This turn is relative to the camera's Z axis. By generating a view straight ahead, then one each from Port and Strbrd, three views can be wrapped around the viewer and a real 3-D effect is generated. (Remember the discussion on OmniMax in Chapter 4?) If the Wide button is turned on and the three views are generated, there will be a seamless interface between the images, giving the illusion that the image is wrapped around your head.

1. Run Vistapro.
2. Set SeaLvl to 100, answer *yes* to the "delete rivers and lakes" dialog box, and answer *yes* to the "generate waves?" dialog box.
3. Make sure Sky, Horizn, Valley, and Cliffs are turned on.
4. Click on River, click near location 2220,120 on the topographic map, and accept the river.
5. Select IQ Script MED from the IQ menu.
6. Set Poly size to 2.
7. Set PDithr to 200.

Left and Right are for generating stereo pairs. Using the value from CamSep to make its calculations, Vistapro adjusts the camera to the left or right by half the value of CamSep. In other words, if CamSep is 10 meters, Left moves the camera left 5 meters and Right moves it right 5 meters. To generate a stereo pair, just generate one image with Left turned on and one with Right turned on. These two images are the stereo pair. Vistapro also has the ability to load these two images back in and generate a grayscale anaglyph; however, because the save functionality is turned off, you cannot do it with this demo version. By saving the two images in 24-bit format and using some of the techniques described in Chapter 6, you can generate a color anaglyph as well.

If you have the full version of Vistapro and you want to generate an anaglyph, ImgSep is important as well. This tells Vistapro how much overlap you want, measured in pixels, when the image is composited. The Load Stereo function loads each respective image and converts them to gray scale, then filters them to red and blue and combines them. ImgSep tells Vistapro how many blank pixels to trim off the edges so that there won't be confusion at the overlap. A negative number in ImgSep pushes the image into the screen instead of projecting it toward you. This can be very entertaining, but it is not very realistic.

Frac

The Fractal panel is where you can have much fun with Vistapro. With it, you can generate an unlimited number of landscapes. The ability to do this is limited in the demo version, however. This tutorial shows you how to use all the functions in this section; however, only one fractal landscape is available—the one having value 1. A value of 0 is the default DEM, which in this case is Yosemite.

The Random button generates a large random number which is automatically used to generate the new landscape. In this version, it always results in either 1 or 0. But in the full version, there are more than 4 billion possibilities. For now, just ignore this button and click in the region below it and enter a 1.

Click the Render button to see what you have created. Remember that the settings are for a fast scene, so set Poly to 1 and texture to L and render again. The particular view we set was for the Yosemite landscape, but it happens to provide an interesting view here as well.

The Island button sets the sea level to the highest value found at the perimeter of your fractal landscape, thus making it look like an island. Click the Island button, then click in the region below and press Enter. Notice the changes in the topographic map. Your land

HANDS-ON WITH VISTAPRO

mass is now surrounded by green. Non-island landscapes are referred to as *floating* landscapes and appear to continue off the edge of the map, as though they were clipped out of a larger region of land. *Island* landscapes are self-contained land masses.

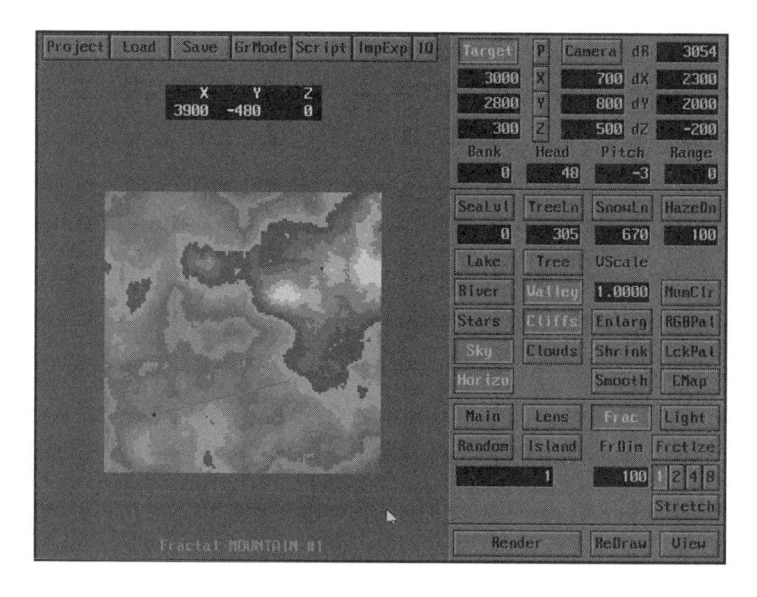

Figure 10.14

Fractal Landscape 1.

FrDim controls the fractal dimension of the mountains. This results in variations in the height and roughness of the landscape. Larger values generate taller, rougher mountains, whereas lower numbers generate flatter, smoother landscapes.

The row of buttons under Frctlze are the fractal divisor buttons. The value tells Vistapro how large the features of the new landscape should be when it is generating one. A small number (such as 1) results in a few large mountains, and a large number (such as 8) results in many smaller mountains. For some fun, click on 8, then click in the region under Random and press Enter. Click the Render button to see the different landscape you have created. You will notice that all the mountains are lower, and that there are more of them.

The Frctlze button adds fractal detail to the existing landscape. Every time you click this button, the value of FrDim is applied to the current landscape. The fractal divisor buttons contribute in that they control the scale at which fractalization occurs. For example, a

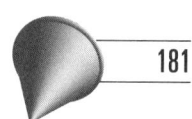

III 3-D COMPUTER APPLICATIONS

large number fractalizes only at small scales, resulting in the same shape landscape, but with a rougher look. A small number changes the shape of mountains.

The Stretch button allows you to stretch the existing features of mountains vertically. A large fractal divisor value stretches only the large masses and a small value stretches only the lower elevations. Stretch can be repeated over and over again for very interesting effects that resemble a caricature of the original land mass.

With all the options in Frac, an infinite number of possible landscapes is possible. With the real version of Vistapro, you can save these creations for use later.

Light

The Light panel controls the lighting of your scene. Click on the Light button. At the left of the panel are buttons labeled *N*, *S*, *E*, and *W*. Clicking one of these quickly sets the light origination direction to North, South, East, or West. The default for this landscape is West.

The length of the line protruding to the West on the panel is an indicator of the declination, or angle, of the light. A long line means the sun is low on the horizon, whereas a short one means it is overhead. These values are also reflected in the boxes to the right of the buttons.

To set a custom value for light, click the Custom button, then go to the topographic map and click where you want the sun to come from. Remember that the closer to the center of the circles, the more directly overhead the sun will be. When you have set the sun, click on the Render button. Notice the difference in shadows and intensity. Notice also that the values for azimuth and declination have changed.

The Rough value at the far right adds a random number to the lighting model so that roughness will appear on the polygons as they are rendered. This is also referred to as *jitter*. Quite often in computer-generated images, a perfect mathematical model looks exactly like that, perfect! Jitter tells the renderer that we want those colors, but altered with this slight aberration. The result is more realistic.

HANDS-ON WITH VISTAPRO

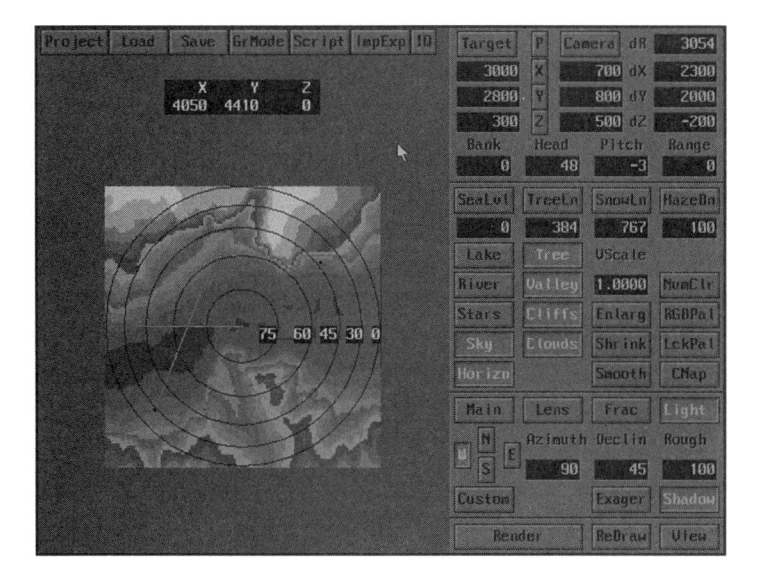

Figure 10.15
The Light controls.

The Exager button sets the exaggerated shading model. Exaggeration is the degree at which shadows fall. If exaggeration is set on, dark areas will get dark faster than if it is set off. This helps to accentuate cliff sides and rocky areas where you want high granularity.

The Shadow button tells Vistapro to cast shadows from cliffs and natural surroundings. Trees are not shadowed. Without shadows, you will still get light and dark areas due to the amount of light cast on the area from the sun; however, with low-angle light, it helps to add shadows for a more dramatic effect.

Summary

As you probably realize by now, Vistapro is an incredibly powerful software package. There are so many options and parameters that virtually any landscape can be generated, modified, and rendered. Extensive animation sequences and elaborate 3-D mechanisms make it one of the most entertaining packages available. Learning about the world of 3-D fractals is fun and educational. This demo version of the software provides just an overview of what is available. Hopefully, your adventures into the world of 3-D can begin in the landscapes of Vistapro. And there's no end in sight!

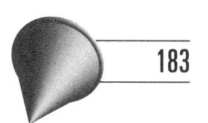

Various References on 3-D

The following references were used in the creation of *Adventures in 3-D*. There are groups and societies, products, catalogs, and books to help further your knowledge and understanding of the topics covered in this book.

Organizations

United States

National Stereoscopic Association
P.O. Box 15801
Columbus, OH 11357

Stereoscopic Society
42922 Woodley Avenue
Wesleyville, PA 16501

APPENDIX A

International

International Stereoscopic Union
P.O. Box 2319
CH-3001 Bern
Switzerland

Catalogs, Products, and Services

Catalog of 3-D Products

Reel 3-D Enterprises
P.O. Box 2368
Culver City, CA 90231

CD-ROM—More than 250 Stereo and Anaglyph Images on Computer

World of GRAFX—3-D Imagery
GRAFX Group, Inc.
1046A Calle Recodo
San Clemente, CA 92673

Equipment and Consulting for 3-D TV

Three-D Video Corporation
4382 Lankershim Boulevard
North Hollywood, CA 91602

Stereo Computer Equipment and Systems

StereoGraphics Corporation
2171-H East Francisco Boulevard
San Rafael, CA 94901

Single-Image, Random-Dot Stereograms

NE Thing Enterprises
19A Crosby Drive
Bedford, MA 01730

3-D Photography Archives and History

California Museum of Photography
University of California, Riverside
Riverside, CA 92521

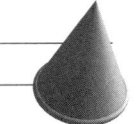

VARIOUS REFERENCES ON 3-D

3-D Glasses and Low-Budget Films

Stereovision International
3421 W. Burbank Blvd.
Burbank, CA 91505

3-D Software Utilities

Schreiber Instruments, Inc.
4800 Happy Canyon Road, Suite 250
Denver, CO 80237
(303) 759-1024

Books on 3-D and Computer Graphics

3-D Photography and Slide Mounting

The World of 3-D
Jac G. Ferwerda
3-D Book Productions
ISBN: 90-71377-51-2

3-D Computer Graphics

Fundamentals of Interactive Computer Graphics
J.D. Foley and A. Van Dam
Addison Wesley
ISBN: 0-201-14468-9

Computer Graphics Programming

Computer Graphics—A Programming Approach
Steven Harrington
McGraw-Hill
ISBN: 0-07-026751-0

Index

24-bit images, 95
3-D computer games
  (Wolfenstein 3-D), 137-146
3-D computer models
  ray tracing, 84-87
  shading, 77-83
  shadows, 83-84
  surface details, 87-91
  translucent/transparent
    materials, 84
3-D images
  computer-generated,
    environmental effects, 91
  holographic, 52-53
  polarized, 50-52
  Pulfrich effect, 54-56
  translating 3-D into 2-D, 72-77
3-D landscape visualization
  program, Vistapro, 149-152
3-D modeling/rendering
  programs, 75, 96
  designing anaglyphs, 97-98
  techniques, 97
3-D photography, 34-36
  aerial photogrammetry, 57-58
  architecture, 61
  biology, 64-66
  entertainment, 62-64
  medical field, 58-60
  military, 62
  space, 66-67
3-D vision, 8-11
  color blindness, 24-25
  environmental conditions, 25
  impaired vision, 24
  visual cues, 8-9
3-D Studio (Autodesk), 91, 96

A

Abbott, Edwin, 2
  Flatland, 18
accommodation of eyes, 21-22
additive fashion, combining
  colors, 98
aerial photogrammetry, 57-58
  military applications, 62
aliased edge, 109
aliasing, 76
amblyopia, 24
Anadraw, 98-103
anaglyph glasses, 94
anaglyph images, 48-50
anaglyphs, 93
  Anadraw, 98-103
  computer screens, 94-95

designing, 97-98
   techniques for 3-D modeling/
     rendering programs, 97
   viewing, 95-96
     with animation, 103-106
anatomy of eyes, 19-23
angle of incidence, 77
animating anaglyphs, 103-106
antialiasing, 110, 178
applications for 3-D photography
   aerial photogrammetry, 57-58
   architecture, 61
   biology, 64-66
   entertainment, 62-64
   medical field, 58-60
   military, 62
   space, 66-67
architecture, 3-D photography, 61
Autodesk Animator Pro, 91

B

backplane removal, 75
beam splitter, 59
binocular vision, 8-11, 47-48
biology, 3-D photography, 64-66
black-and-white stereo pairs, 97
books, 3-D/computer graphics, 187
Brewster, Sir David, 31, 34
Brewster Stereoscope, 31
bump mapping, 88

C

California Museum of Photography, 186
cameras
   stereo, 34-38
   Vistapro, 157-161
Cantor bar, 122-124
Cantor, Georg, 122
catalogs, 3-D/computer graphics, 186-187
color blindness, 24-25
color reduction, 95

colors, combining, additive/
   subtractive techniques, 98
commands, macro, 95
CompuServe, GIF (Graphics Interchange Format) files, 113
computer games
   3-D, 63-64
   technology, 137-138
   Wolfenstein 3-D, 138-146
Computer Graphics—A Programming Approach, 187
computer models
   programs, 75
   ray tracing, 84-87
   shading, 77-83
   shadows, 83-84
   surface details, 87-91
   translucent/transparent materials, 84
computer screens
   anaglyphs, 94-106
   translating 3-D into 2-D, 72-77
computer-generated 3-D images, environmental effects, 91
computers, virtual reality, 128-129
   applications, 131-132
   input/output devices, 129-131
cones, 24
convergence of eyes, 21-23
converging objects, 11
cross-eyed viewing, 44
Crystal Eyes (StereoGraphics Corporation) systems, 119
cubic environment mapping, 89-90
cyclopean vision, *see* binocular vision

D

depth perception, 8
designing anaglyphs, 97-98
diffuse reflection, 82-83
Digital Elevation Model files, 150-151
digital image processing, 94-95

INDEX

direction of propagation of light, 50, 54
drawing stereo pairs, 114-117
drawing styles
   isometric, 15
   perspective, 15-18

E

education
   fractal technology, 126
   virtual reality, 132
effects, monocular, 9
entertainment, 3-D photography, 62-64
environmental conditions effect on vision, 25
Erskine shift technique, 38, 96
Erskine, Stephen, 38, 95-96
Escher, M.C., 15
Euclidean geometry, 121
experience, relative size, 11-13
eyes
   anatomy, 19-23
   images, 7-8
   rods, 24

F

faces, 77
field framing, 55
files
   Digital Elevation Model, 150-151
   GIF (Graphics Interchange Format), 113
flat shading of computer models, 77-79
Flatland, 2
   Edwin Abbott, 18
focal point, 28-32
fovea centralis, 23
Frac panel (Vistapro), 180-182
fractal geometry, 121-127

fractals
   background/history, 121-124
   technology
      generating landscapes, 87, 150
      simulations, 124-127
freeware files, PICEM.EXE, 95-96, 113-114
Fuhrmann, A., Welt-Panorama Zentrale, 34
Fundamentals of Interactive Computer Graphics, 187

G

games, *see* computer games
geometry
   Euclidean, 121
   fractal, 121-127
GIF (Graphics Interchange Format) files, 113
Gouraud, H., 79
   shading of computer models, 79
graphics hardware, 108-110
GrMode menu (Vistapro), 155
Gruber, Wilhelm, 36

H

hand-held lens stereoscopes, 45
hardware
   graphics, 108-110
   requirements for Vistapro, 150
   stereo viewing devices
      Crystal Eyes (StereoGraphics Corporation), 119
      LCD shutter glasses, 118-119
helium-neon lasers, 52
Holmes, Oliver Wendell, 31
Holmes Stereoscope, 31, 46
holographic 3-D images, 52-53
hypo-stereo images, 64, 110-112

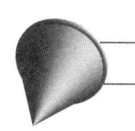

191

I

IBM-compatible VGA (Video Graphics Array) system, 118
image processing, digital, 94-95
images
   3-D
      holographic, 52-53
      polarized, 50-52
      Pulfrich effect, 54-56
   anaglyph, 48-50
   computer generated 3-D
      environmental effects, 91
      ray tracing, 84-87
      shading, 77-83
      shadows, 83-84
      surface details, 87-91
      transparent/translucent materials, 84
   cyclopean, 47-48
   eyes, 7-8
   hypo-stereo, 110-112
   planar, 42
   quality, 10
   two-color, 95
immersion, 128
impaired vision, 24
ImpExp menu (Vistapro), 155
input/output devices, virtual reality, 129-131
interference patterns, 52
International Stereoscopic Union, 186
IQ menu (Vistapro), 156
isometric drawing style, 15

J-L

jitters, 182
Julesz, Bela, 47-48

Kaiser Panorama, 34

lasers, helium-neon, 52
lateral geniculate body, 21
lazy eye, 24
LCD shutter glasses, 118-119
LCD shutter technology, 63
Lens panel (Vistapro), 178-180
lens stereoscopes, 28-32
   hand-held, 45
   self-standing, 46
lenticular photography, Nimslo, 38
light
   monochromatic, 52
   polarized, 51
   propagation, 50, 54
Light panel (Vistapro), 182-183
linear sets, numbers, 123
Lo, Allen, 38
Load menu (Vistapro), 155
London Stereoscopic Company, 35

M

macro
   commands, 95
   stereoscopy, 64
magnetic resonance imaging (MRI), 60
Main panel (Vistapro), 176-178
Mandelbrot, Benoit, 123
mapping
   bump, 88
   coordinates, 87
   cubic environment, 89-90
   fractal technology, 124-126
   opacity, 90
   reflectance, 89
   texture, 87
medical field
   3-D photography, 58-60
   virtual reality, 131
memory, virtual, 127
menus, Vistapro, 155-156
microbes, 65
microscopic stereo images, 65
military, 3-D photography, 62
modeling programs, computer, 75
models, computer
   ray tracing, 84-87
   shading, 77-83

INDEX

shadows, 83-84
surface details, 87-91
translucent/transparent materials, 84
monitors, 108-110
monochromatic light, 52
monocular
   effects, 9
   zones, 23
movies, 3-D, 62-63

N

NASA, 66
National Stereoscopic Association, 185
NE Thing Enterprises, 48, 186
night blindness, 24
Nims, Jerry, 38
numbers linear/nonlinear sets, 123

O

objects, 11
   Vistapro, 162
      cliffs, 164-165
      clouds, 170-172
      haze density, 164
      lakes, 165-167
      rivers, 165-167
      sea level, 162
      skies, 164-165
      snow lines, 163
      stars, 168
      tree lines, 163
      trees, 168-170
      valleys, 164-165
OmniMax theater, 63
one-point perspective
   drawing, 17
   projection, 73
opacity mapping, 90
optic cup, 60
optic nerve ending, 23
optical illusion, 15
organizations, 3-D/computer graphics, 185

P-Q

page-flipping, 104
parallel
   projection, 74
   viewing, 42-44
peripheral vision, 16
perspective
   drawing style, 15-18
   projection, 73-74
   viewing (Vistapro), 159-160
petrochemical industry, aerial photogrammetry, 58
Phong Bui-Tuong, 80
Phong shading of computer models, 80-81
photogrammetry, aerial, 57-58
photography, 34-36
   3-D
      aerial photogrammetry, 57-58
      architecture, 61
      biology, 64-66
      entertainment applications, 62-64
      medical field, 58-60
      military applications, 62
      space, 66-67
   Nimslo lenticular, 38
   stereo, 34-38
PICEM.EXE file, 95-96, 113-114
pixel dither, 177
pixels, 75
planar images, 42
points, registration, 11
polarized
   3-D images, 50-52
   light, 51
polylines, 104
problems with vision
   color blindness, 24-25
   environmental conditions, 25
   impaired vision, 24
products, 3-D/computer graphics, 186-187
programs
   3-D modeling/rendering, 96
      designing anaglyphs, 97-98
      techniques, 97

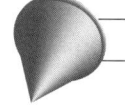

3D Studio (Autodesk), 96
Anadraw, 98-103
computer modeling, 75
STEREO (Schreiber
 Instruments), 103-106
STEREOD, 114-117
SURF3D (Schreiber
 Instruments), 106
Vistapro, 149-161, 176-183
Wolfenstein 3-D, 137-146
Project menu (Vistapro), 155
projection plane, 73
propagation of light, 50, 54
Pulfrich effect, 54-56

R

random-dot stereograms, 23,
 47-48
ray tracing, 84-87
Reel 3-D Enterprises, 46, 186
reflectance mapping, 89
reflecting stereoscopes, 27-28,
 32-34, 46-47
reflections, diffuse/specular, 82-83
refraction
 calculating, ray tracing, 84-87
 transparent/translucent
  materials, 84
registration points, 11
relative size, 11-13
relaxed stereo viewing, 42-44
rendering, Vistapro, 176-183
resolution/color graphics, 108-110
retina, 20
retinal disparity, 22-23
rods in eyes, 24

S

Save menu (Vistapro), 155
scanning technologies, 60
Schreiber Instruments, Inc., 187
sciences, virtual technology, 131
scope of vision, 14-19
Script menu (Vistapro), 155

Sega, 3-D games, 63
self-standing lens stereoscope, 46
senses, virtual reality, 129
services, 3-D/computer graphics,
 186-187
shading, computer models, 77
 diffuse and specular reflection,
  82-83
 flat, 77-79
 Gouraud, 79
 Phong, 80-81
shadows, computer models, 83-84
simulations, fractal technology,
 124-127
sizes, relative, 11-13
snow-blindness, 24
software
 Anadraw, 98-103
 files, PICEM.EXE, 95-96
 STEREO (Schreiber
  Instruments), 103-106
 STEREOD, 114-117
 SURF3D (Schreiber
  Instruments), 106
 Vistapro, 149-183
 see also programs
sonograms, 3-D, 60
space, 3-D photography, 66-67
specular highlights, 82-83
starting
 Vistapro, 152-154
 Wolfenstein 3-D, 139
STEREO (Schreiber Instruments),
 103-106
stereo cameras, 34-38
stereo microscopy, 110
stereo pairs, 41-48, 110-111
 black-and-white, 97
 drawing, 114-117
 separating images, 111-112
 viewing, 112-114
  Crystal Eyes (StereoGraphics
   Corporation), 119
  LCD shutter glasses, 118-119
stereo photography, *see* 3-D
 photography
stereo viewing, 42-44

INDEX

STEREO.EXE file, 104-105
STEREOD, 114-117
stereograms, random-dot, 47-48
StereoGraphics Corporation, 186
   Crystal Eyes, 119
stereoscopes
   Brewster, 31
   Holmes, 31, 46
   Kaiser Panorama, 34
   lens, 28-32
      hand-held, 45
      self-standing, 46
   reflecting, 27-28, 32-34, 46-47
   Wild ST4 Mirror, 33
Stereoscopic Society, 185
Stereovision International, 187
structure of eyes, 20-21
subatomic particles, 65
subtractive fashion, combining colors, 98
SURF3D (Schreiber Instruments), 106
surface normal, 77

T-U

targets (Vistapro), 156-157
texture mapping, 87
Three-D Video Corporation, 186
three-point perspective projection, 74
tiling, texture mapping, 88
translucent materials, 84
transparent materials, 84
triangulation, 58
true-color images, 95

V

VCH reflecting stereoscopes, 46
vertices, 77
viewing
   anaglyphs, 95-96
      with animation, 103-106
   stereo, relaxed, 42-44
   stereo pairs, 112-114
      Crystal Eyes (StereoGraphics Corporation), 119
      LCD shutter glasses, 118-119
Viewmaster, 36
views, Vistapro, 156-161
virtual memory, 127
virtual reality
   applications, 131-132
   background/history, 127-128
   computers, 128-129
   input/output devices, 129-131
vision
   binocular, 8-11
   cues, 18-20
   impaired, 24
   peripheral, 16
   three-dimensional, 8, 9-11
   see also 3-D vision
Vistapro, 149-150
   applications, 150-151
   data sources, 151
   hardware requirements, 150
   improving rendering, 176-183
   installing/starting, 152-154
   maximum utilization, 152
   menus, 155-156
   models, 172-175
   objects, 162
      cliffs, 164-165
      clouds, 170-172
      haze density, 164
      horizons, 164-165
      lakes, 165-167
      rivers, 165-167
      sea level, 162
      snow lines, 163
      stars, 168
      tree lines, 163
      trees, 168-170
      valleys, 164-165
   selecting views, 156-161
visual cortex, 21
visual cues, 3-D vision, 8-9

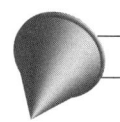

W-Z

Walt Disney Corporation, 63
Walton, Bill C., 62
Watson Research Institute, 123
wave-particle duality of light, 50
Welt-Panorama Zentrale, 34
Wheatstone, Sir Charles, 27
Wild ST4 Mirror Stereoscope, 33
Wolfenstein 3-D (ID Software), 137-138
   armament, 141
   game details, 142
   hints, 146
   keys for tasks, 142-144
   killing enemies, 141, 145-146
   movement, 140
   opening doors/elevators, 141
   scenario, 138-139
   starting, 139-140
   status screen, 144-145
The World of 3-D, 187
World of GRAFX—3-D Imagery, 186

Z-buffering, 75

ANNOUNCING VISTAPRO 3.0!

VIRTUAL REALITY LANDSCAPE GENERATION SOFTWARE

Mount St. Helens, Washington

Inside this book, you'll find a demo copy of Vistapro 3.0, the incredible virtual reality landscape generator based on real-world data obtained from the U.S. Geological Survey and NASA.

Once you've tried our demo of Vistapro 3.0, with its 24-Bit color, 3-D trees, fractal texturing and clouds, we're sure you'll be ready for the real thing! Unlike the demo, the full version of Vistapro 3.0 is loaded with features which allow you to:

- Explore 19 different landscape sets of earth and Mars, (many more available separately!) or explore billions of imaginary fractal places ● Have FULL CONTROL over trees and clouds ● LOAD AND SAVE your creations in a variety of formats (Supports 24-bit BMP, Targa 24, PCX and FLC (Autodesk animation) ● Generate left and right images for 3-D viewing (includes 3-D glasses and pre-rendered 3-D images and a tutorial) ● Render images larger than 640 x 480 ● Load larger landscapes and multiple contiguous landscapes ● **AND MORE!**

Yosemite National Park, California

Mail orders or inquiries to:
2341 Ganador Court, San Luis Obispo, CA 93401
(805) 545-8515 FAX (805) 781-2259
Also available for Amiga. Macintosh available in Summer 1993

Order Today and Save $30
off the retail price of $129.95!

YES! I want to become a virtual explorer! Please send me Vistapro 3.0 IBM for only $99.95 plus shipping.

Name_____
Address_____
City_____
State/Province_____Zip/PC_____
Country_____Phone_____
☐ VISA ☐ Mastercard #_____
Exp._____Signature_____

SHIPPING: Please add $5.00 shipping/handling inside the continental U.S. for a total of $104.95. Add $10.00 shipping/handling outside the continental U.S. for a total of $109.95.

Virtual Reality Laboratories, Inc. 1-800-829-VRLI

Software Installation Instructions

The software included with this book is easy to install on your system. It must be installed on your hard disk in order to run.

System Requirements

IBM-compatible computer (80386 or better for Vistapro)

VGA graphics and monitor (VESA SVGA is optional for Vistapro)

4M RAM

At least 3M free hard disk space

Mouse (required for Vistapro)

> **Note:** The install program that decompresses the software to your hard disk makes the required directories and copies all the software. If you want to move the software to some other directory after it is installed, feel free to do so. None of the software is directory-dependent.

Installation

To install the software follow these steps:

1. Insert the disk in drive A or B.
2. Type A:INSTALL (or B:INSTALL if you put the disk in drive B).

The program automatically puts the six different software pieces into six different directories under the main directory, QUE3D. After installation, your hard disk looks like this:

```
C:\
    QUE3D\
            3DPICS\
            ANADRAW\
            STEREO\
            STEREOD\
            VP\
            WOLF3D\
```

If you have more than one hard disk (logical or physical), you can specify a different disk on which to install the software by typing

```
A:INSTALL x:
```

in which *x* is the letter of the installation drive.

Disclaimer

By opening this package, you are agreeing to be bound by the following:

This software product is copyrighted, and all rights are reserved by the publisher and author. You are licensed to use this software on a single computer. You may copy and/or modify the software as needed to facilitate your use of it on a single computer. Making copies of the software for any other purpose is a violation of the United States copyright laws.

This software is sold *as is* without warranty of any kind, either expressed or implied, including but not limited to the implied warranties of merchantability and fitness for a particular purpose. Neither the publisher nor its dealers or distributors assumes any liability for any alleged or actual damages arising from the use of this program. (Some states do not allow for the exclusion of implied warranties, so the exclusion may not apply to you.)